THE LATER YEARS

Student Practice Workbook

Gibbs Smith, Publisher
INSPIRING STUDENTS. REINVENTING TEXTBOOKS.
Salt Lake City | Charleston | Santa Fe | Santa Barbara

Copyright ©2008 by Gibbs Smith, Publisher

Text, maps, graphs, and drawings ©2008 by Gibbs Smith, Publisher

All rights reserved. No part of this book, with the exception of the Student Worksheets and Chapter Tests, may be reproduced or transmitted by any means, either mechanical or electronic, without written permission from the publisher.

Published by:

Gibbs Smith, Publisher
P.O. Box 667
Layton, UT 84041

Phone: (800) 748-5439
Fax: (800) 213-3023
E-mail: textbooks@gibbs-smith.com
Internet: www.gibbs-smith.com/textbooks

Written by Rachel Pike
Editorial Assistance by Jen Petersen
Designed by Alan Connell
Cover designed by Alan Connell
Printed in the U.S.A.

ISBN 978-1-4236-0515-7

Table of Contents

Chapter 1 1

Chapter 2 19

Chapter 3 37

Chapter 4 57

Chapter 5 75

Chapter 6 95

Chapter 7 115

Chapter 8 133

Chapter 9 151

Chapter 10 167

Chapter 1
Tennessee: The Place We Call Home (Student Edition pp. 2-31)

Table of Contents			
Activity Master	Standard Correlation	Page #	Accompanies Student Edition pages
Scavenger Hunt	5.3.spi.1	2-3	Entire textbook
Lesson 1 Reading Guide	5.3.spi.1, 5.3.spi.6	4-7	4-11
Lesson 2 Reading Guide	5.3.spi.7	8-11	12-16
Passport to History	5.3.spi.8	12	14
Lesson 3 Reading Guide	5.3.spi.7	13-15	17-29
Grand Divisions	5.3.spi.7	16	17
ELL: Landforms and Regions	5.3. spi.7	17	2-31
Chapter Review	5.3.spi.4, 5.3.spi.5, 5.3.spi.7, 5.3.spi.8	18	2-31

© 2008 Gibbs Smith, Publisher
Accompanies *Tennessee Through Time: The Later Years*

Name _____   Date _____

CHAPTER 1 ACTIVITY MASTER

Scavenger Hunt (Page 1)

Objective: 5.3.spi.1
Accompanies Student Edition entire textbook

Directions: Use your textbook to locate and answer the questions.

Title of Book: _____
Author: _____
Publisher: _____
Copyright Date: _____

1. Where is the Table of Contents located, and what is its purpose?
   _____

2. Locate Chapter 10 in the Table of Contents. What topic does this chapter cover, and on what pages is it located?
   _____

3. Use the Index as a reference to complete the chart.

Person or Event	Page Numbers	Fact About Person or Event
Samuel Gompers		
Butler Act		
New Deal		
Sequoyah		
Minnie Pearl		

4. Locate the timeline in Chapter 6. On what date did Garnet and Frieda Carter open Rock City?
   _____

5. Examine the bar graph on p. 121. What is the title of the bar graph?
   _____

6. In which chapter will you learn about the Declaration of Independence?
   _____

© 2008 Gibbs Smith, Publisher
Accompanies *Tennessee Through Time: The Later Years*

Name _____   Date _____

CHAPTER 1 ACTIVITY MASTER

Scavenger Hunt (Page 2)

Directions: Use your textbook to locate and answer the questions.

7. On which pages would you find a map of the world?
   _____

8. What do pp. 54-55, 178-179, and 252-253 all have in common?
   _____

9. In which chapter and lesson would you find information about America entering World War II?
   _____

10. Whose picture is on p. 192?
    _____

11. Using information on p. 336, identify the three branches of the national government and the state government officials for each branch.
    _____

12. Study the map on p. 306, and name the countries that border Vietnam.
    _____

13. Use the map on p. 227 to identify the two oceans that border the United States.
    _____

14. What type of artifact can be seen on p. 114?
    _____

15. What do pp. 21, 146, and 308 have in common?
    _____

16. Study the pictures or photographs that introduce each chapter. Select one picture or photograph and write a short description of what you think is happening.
    _____

17. "Words to Understand" begin each lesson. Turn to one example. How are the words organized?
    _____

18. How would you describe the organization of this book?
    _____

© 2008 Gibbs Smith, Publisher
Accompanies *Tennessee Through Time: The Later Years*

Name _____   Date _____

CHAPTER 1 ACTIVITY MASTER

Lesson 1 Reading Guide (Page 1)

Objectives: 5.3.spi.1, 5.3.spi.6
Accompanies Student Edition pp. 4-11

Part I: Vocabulary

Directions: Fill in the chart using the six vocabulary words from Lesson 1. Write in the page number where it is found in Lesson 1.

Word	Definition	Page Number	Example sentence in your own words
1. atlas entry			
2. boundary			
3. continent			
4. grid			
5. physical boundary			
6. political boundary			

Part II: Places to Locate

Directions: Describe the location of each place in relation to Tennessee using all the maps in Lesson 1.

Example: "Africa" Africa is a continent east of Tennessee across the Atlantic Ocean.

1. Appalachian Mountains

_____

_____

2. Atlantic Ocean

_____

_____

Name _____ Date _____

CHAPTER 1 ACTIVITY MASTER

Lesson 1 Reading Guide (Page 2)

3. Canada
_____
_____

4. Mexico
_____
_____

5. Mississippi River
_____
_____

6. North America
_____
_____

7. Pacific Ocean
_____
_____

Part III: Headings

Directions: Write in the headings and subheadings from Lesson 1 starting with the title of the lesson.

1. Title p. 4 _____
2. Heading p. 4 _____
3. Heading p. 5 _____
4. Heading p. 6 _____
5. Heading p. 9 _____
6. Subheading p. 9 _____
7. Subheading p. 9 _____
8. Subheading p. 10 _____

© 2008 Gibbs Smith, Publisher
Accompanies *Tennessee Through Time: The Later Years*

Name _____ Date _____

CHAPTER 1 ACTIVITY MASTER

Lesson 1 Reading Guide (Page 3)

Part IV: Short Answer

Directions: Answer the questions in complete sentences.

1. Look at the photograph on p. 4. What is going on in the picture?
   _____
   _____

2. Name the seven continents (map p. 5).
   _____
   _____

3. What is outlined in white on the map on p. 7?
   _____
   _____

4. How would you recognize the difference between physical and political boundaries (p. 9)?
   _____
   _____

5. What is another use for a grid besides a map of Tennessee?
   _____
   _____

Part V: Memory Master

1. Tennessee lies on which continent?
   _____

2. What is a political boundary?
   _____

3. How can an atlas entry help us find a place?
   _____

Name _____   Date _____

CHAPTER 1 ACTIVITY MASTER

Lesson 1 Reading Guide (Page 4)

Part VI: Constructed Response

Directions: Answer the question using critical thinking skills.

How do all the maps in Lesson 1 help you study Tennessee history?

_____

_____

_____

_____

_____

Part VII: Note Home

Lesson 1 Reading Guide is a basic overview of what the students have learned in Chapter 1 pp. 4-11. The Memory Master questions and the Constructed Response are indicators of student comprehension. For supplemental activities, see experiencestatehistory.com and click on Tennessee. Check with the teacher for the student login password.

Name _____ Date _____

CHAPTER 1 ACTIVITY MASTER

Lesson 2 Reading Guide (Page 1)

Objective: 5.3.spi.7
Accompanies Student Edition pp. 12-16

Part I: Vocabulary

Directions: Read the definition, then fill in the blank with the correct vocabulary word.

1. inland; away from the coast _____

2. rain or snow _____

3. the study of the earth and the people, animals, and plants living on it _____

4. containing a high amount of water or water vapor _____

5. a graph that charts information about a particular location's climate _____

6. something found in nature that people use _____

7. a natural feature on the earth's surface _____

8. made by people _____

9. the day-to-day temperature, precipitation, and pressure of a place _____

10. how high a place is above sea level _____

11. the pattern of weather of a place _____

Hinky Pinkies

Directions: Hinky Pinkies are clues where the answer is two words that rhyme. Create a Hinky Pinky using a vocabulary word. A non-vocabulary word example has been done for you.

Example: What do you call a container full of stones? Answer: rocks box

12. Question: _____

    Answer: _____

Lesson 2 Reading Guide (Page 2)

Part II: Places to Locate

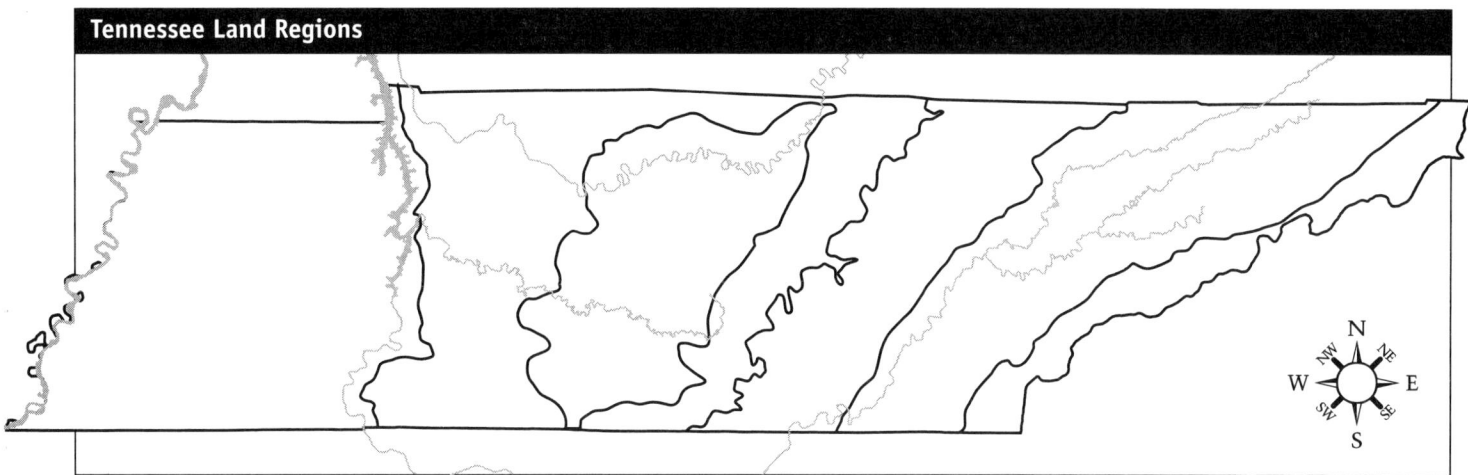

Directions: Label the map with the correct locations using the numbers in the word bank. Try to see how many you can do without looking at the map in your book on pp. 12-13. Then use the map to check your work.

1. Cumberland Plateau	3. West Tennessee Plain	6. Highland Rim	9. Tennessee River
2. Great Smoky Mountains	4. Duck River	7. Great Valley	10. Cumberland River
	5. Mississippi River	8. Central Basin	

Name _____   Date _____

CHAPTER 1 ACTIVITY MASTER

Lesson 2 Reading Guide (Page 3)

Part III: Short Answer

Directions: Answer the questions in complete sentences using your textbook.

1. How is Tennessee's geography diverse?
   _____
   _____

2. In which land region do you live?
   _____
   _____

3. If our state were a shape in geometry, how would you describe it?
   _____
   _____

4. How would you describe Tennessee's location in relation to the equator?
   _____
   _____

5. How does elevation affect the climate?
   _____
   _____

6. Predict what life would be like without natural resources.
   _____
   _____

Part IV: Memory Master

1. What are the parts of a place's geography?
   _____

2. Name three land regions in Tennessee.
   _____

3. What is a natural resource?
   _____

Name _____ Date _____

CHAPTER 1 ACTIVITY MASTER

Lesson 2 Reading Guide (Page 4)

Part V: Constructed Response

Directions: Answer the questions using critical thinking skills.

Pretend you are a weather reporter (a meteorologist), and write a report of the weather. You can write about today's weather or any other day. Use as many vocabulary words as you can.

_____

_____

_____

_____

_____

Part VI: Note Home

Lesson 2 Reading Guide is a basic overview of what the students have learned in Chapter 1 pp. 12-16. The Memory Master questions and the Constructed Response are indicators of student comprehension. For supplemental activities, see experiencestatehistory.com and click on Tennessee. Check with the teacher for the student login password.

Name _____ Date _____

CHAPTER 1 ACTIVITY MASTER

Passport to History

Objective: 5.3.spi.8
Accompanies Student Edition p. 14

Teacher Initial _____

Date _____

Part I: Create Your Own Climograph

Directions: Track the highest and the lowest temperature each day for 10 days on the graph below. For each day, you will have two bars: one for the high and one for the low temperature. Give your graph a title.

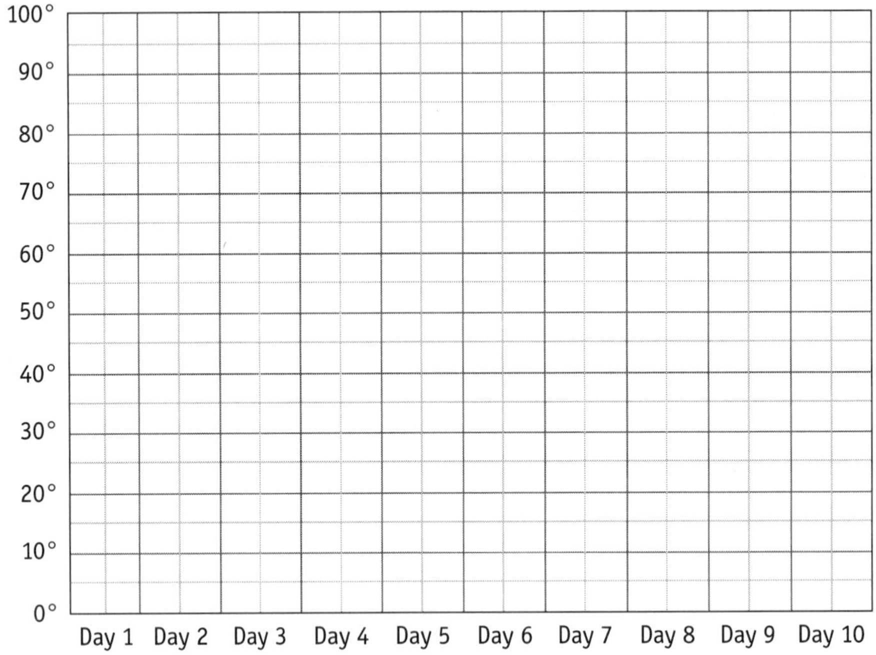

[Graph: Y-axis 0° to 100° in 10° increments; X-axis Day 1 through Day 10]

Part II: Interpret Your Climograph

1. Which day experienced the highest temperature? The lowest? _____
   _____

2. What was the average high temperature over the 10 days. (Hint: Add all 10 high numbers, then divide that number by 10 for the average temperature.) _____
   _____

3. Do you observe any patterns on your chart? _____
   _____

4. Did the temperature make a significant change during the 10 days? _____
   _____

5. Could you make any general statements about the climate in your area this time of year?
   _____

Name _____ Date _____

CHAPTER 1 ACTIVITY MASTER

Lesson 3 Reading Guide (Page 1)

Objective: 5.3.spi.7
Accompanies Student Edition pp. 17-29

Part I: Vocabulary
Directions: Circle the correct answer.

1. A poster has the slogan "West is the Best!" This poster demonstrates which belief?
   A lumbering
   B smelting
   C sectionalism
   D chandelier

2. Chandler's family makes a living with the natural resource ore. What is mostly likely their profession?
   A lumbering
   B smelting
   C sectionalism
   D chandelier

3. Camp Sanderson offers hikes to the tops of the Smoky Mountains. What are you most likely to see there?
   A balds
   B smelting
   C chandelier
   D lumbering

4. Rita's family makes a living with the natural resource wood. What is mostly likely their profession?
   A lumbering
   B smelting
   C sectionalism
   D chandelier

5. During which activity would you be most likely to find Indian artifacts?
   A lumbering in East Tennessee
   B smelting in Middle Tennessee
   C hiking to a cove
   D taking pictures of a chandelier

© 2008 Gibbs Smith, Publisher
Accompanies *Tennessee Through Time: The Later Years*

Name _____   Date _____

CHAPTER 1 ACTIVITY MASTER

Lesson 3 Reading Guide (Page 2)

Part II: Places to Locate

Directions: As you read through Lesson 3, match the description with the correct region. Write the letter of the correct answer in the blank. Some questions have more than one answer.

A. East Tennessee
B. Middle Tennessee
C. West Tennessee

___ 1. Nashville
___ 2. Polk County
___ 3. Central Basin
___ 4. Elk River
___ 5. Tennessee River
___ 6. Great Smoky Mountains
___ 7. Harpeth River
___ 8. Highland Rim
___ 9. Knoxville
___ 10. Memphis
___ 11. Great Valley
___ 12. Duck River
___ 13. Cumberland River
___ 14. Cumberland Plateau
___ 15. Sequatchie Valley

Part III: People to Know

Directions: Fill in the chart about W. C. Handy. Use inference skills for some of the answers.

Year Born—Year Died	
Feelings about jobs	
Feelings about music	
Places lived	
Genre (type) of music	

14

© 2008 Gibbs Smith, Publisher
Accompanies *Tennessee Through Time: The Later Years*

Name _____   Date _____

CHAPTER 1 ACTIVITY MASTER

Lesson 3 Reading Guide (Page 3)

Part IV: Memory Master

1. Describe one landform in East Tennessee.
   _____

2. Describe the climate of Middle Tennessee.
   _____

3. Name one natural resource found in West Tennessee.
   _____

Part V: Constructed Response
Directions: Answer the question using critical thinking skills.

LANDFORMS   CLIMATE   NATURAL RESOURCES

Choose one word above, and describe how Tennessee's three divisions compare. For example, if you pick climate, compare the climate of the three divisions.

_____
_____
_____
_____
_____

Part VI: Note Home

Lesson 3 Reading Guide is a basic overview of what the students have learned in Chapter 1 pp. 17-29. The Memory Master questions and the Constructed Response are indicators of student comprehension. For supplemental activities, see experiencestatehistory.com and click on Tennessee. Check with the teacher for the student login password.

Name _____ Date _____

CHAPTER 1 ACTIVITY MASTER

Grand Divisions

Objective: 5.3.spi.7
Accompanies Student Edition p. 17

Part I: Drawings

Directions: Draw a picture that represents each of the Grand Divisions in the boxes below.

West	Middle	East

Part II: Writing Response

Directions: Write four sentences that describe the division where you live. Include details about climate, landforms, and natural resources.

_____
_____
_____
_____

Part III: Graphic Organizer

Directions: Make a graphic organizer to compare the information about the three Grand Divisions. You may use a chart, diagram, or web to organize the information.

© 2008 Gibbs Smith, Publisher
Accompanies *Tennessee Through Time: The Later Years*

Name _____ Date _____

CHAPTER 1 ACTIVITY MASTER

ELL: Landforms and Regions

Objective: 5.3.spi.7
Accompanies Student Edition pp. 12-16

Part I: Name these landforms.

_____ _____ _____ _____

Part II: Name the three Grand Divisions of Tennessee.

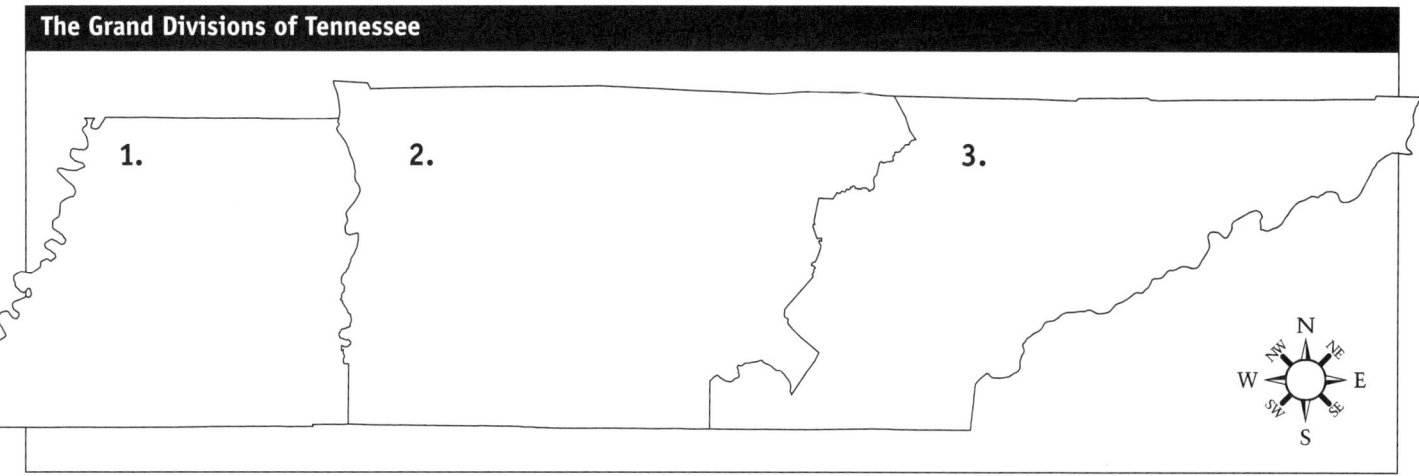

Part III: Name the six land regions of Tennessee.

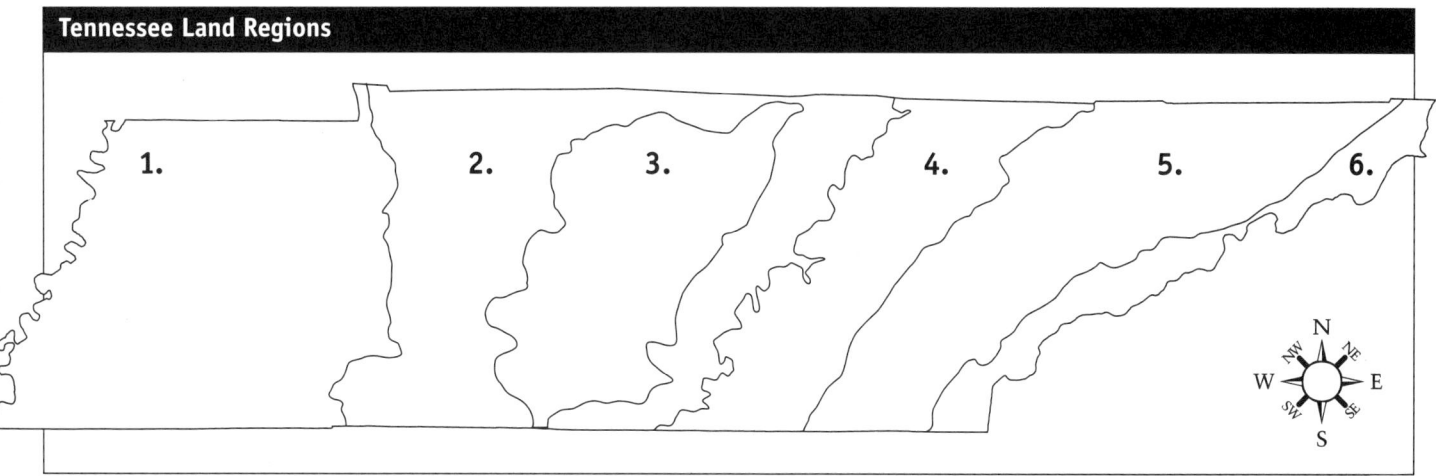

© 2008 Gibbs Smith, Publisher
Accompanies *Tennessee Through Time: The Later Years*

17

Name _____ Date _____

CHAPTER 1 REVIEW

Chapter Review Study Guide

Objectives: 5.3.spi.4, 5.3.spi.5, 5.3.spi.7, 5.3.spi.8
Accompanies Student Edition pp. 2-31

Part I: Vocabulary
Directions: Study the following terms. You may also use your Lesson Reading Guides.

atlas entry	humid	grid	natural resource
political boundary	weather	continental	cove
geography	continent	man-made	lumbering
precipitation	climograph	chandelier	ore
boundary	landform	physical boundary	sectionalism
climate	balds	elevation	smelting

Part II: Review the following ideas for Constructed and Extended Response.
- How would you name all the ways to describe Tennessee's location?
- How does the geography of the United States help us understand things about Tennessee?
- What is the difference between physical and political boundaries?
- Give examples of physical and political boundaries.
- What information does an atlas give?
- How do you find location using latitude and longitude lines?
- How is Tennessee's geography diverse?
- What is the difference between climate and weather?
- Does sectionalism still exist today? Identify ways to solve sectionalism either in the past or today.
- How would you compare climate among the three divisions?
- How would you compare landforms among the three divisions?
- How would you compare natural resources among the three divisions?
- What do you think makes Tennessee a valuable place to live?

Part III: Review
Directions: Use the space below to draw pictures that help you remember the main ideas of Chapter 1.

CHAPTER 2 TABLE OF CONTENTS

Chapter 2
Tennessee's Beginnings (Student Edition pp. 32-55)

	Table of Contents		
Activity Master	Standard Correlation	Page #	Accompanies Student Edition pages
Lesson 1 Reading Guide	5.1.spi.3, 5.6.spi.2	20-28	34-49
Lesson 2 Reading Guide	4.3.spi.5	29-32	50-53
North and South	5.5.spi.1	33	50-51
ELL: Main Ideas	5.1.spi.3, 5.6.spi.2	34	34-49
Chapter Review	4.3.spi.5	35-36	32-55

© 2008 Gibbs Smith, Publisher
Accompanies *Tennessee Through Time: The Later Years*

Lesson 1 Reading Guide (Page 1)

Objectives: 5.1.spi.3, 5.6.spi.2
Accompanies Student Edition pp. 34-49

Part I: Understanding the First People

A. Directions: Read the paragraph below. From your understanding of the textbook pp. 34-35, underline the statements that are false. Then correct the false statements above the line.

The tribes in Tennessee were similar to other North American tribes because each had the same culture. The groups spoke different languages, had the same belief systems, and never fought about land and hunting rights. The Cherokees lived in the Appalachian Mountains along parts of the Mississippi River. They were the largest tribe in the Northeast. The Chickasaws, Creeks, Shawnees, and Yuchis also lived in Kansas and Tennessee.

B. Directions: Apply what you have learned to your own life by trying one of these activities.
1. Demonstrate how to use an atlatl.
2. Read a nonfiction or historical fiction book about the Cherokees, Chickasaws, Creeks, Shawnees, or Yuchis.
3. Eat a farm-grown food that American Indians would have eaten, like fruits, vegetables, and grains.

Name _____   Date _____

CHAPTER 2 ACTIVITY MASTER

Lesson 1 Reading Guide (Page 2)

Part II: Europeans Arrive

A. Directions: Imagine you lived during the time of exploration. Imagine you are understanding this time period from the point of view of the explorer as well as the native. Answer the critical thinking questions from both viewpoints.

1. Why were European nations competing for land?

   European explorer: _____

   _____

   Native: _____

   _____

2. How did life in the New World change with the introduction of new things from Europe?

   European explorer: _____

   _____

   Native: _____

   _____

3. What did you think of the new culture you encountered in the Mississippi River and Tennessee region?

   European explorer: _____

   _____

   Native: _____

   _____

B. Directions: Apply what you have learned to your own life by trying one of these activities.

1. Learn about the specific diseases that killed Native Americans.
2. Find a piece of material or article of clothing that was similar to what Native Americans wore in the 1500s.
3. Draw a picture of the Tennessee River, and label on your picture what natural resources Native Americans used from the river.

© 2008 Gibbs Smith, Publisher
Accompanies *Tennessee Throught Time: The Later Years*

Name _____ Date _____

CHAPTER 2 ACTIVITY MASTER

Lesson 1 Reading Guide (Page 3)

Part III: Thirteen British Colonies

A. Directions: Label the Thirteen Colonies on the map below.

B. Directions: Write two characteristics for each group on the chart.

Southern Colonies	Middle Colonies	New England Colonies

Name _____ Date _____

CHAPTER 2 ACTIVITY MASTER

Lesson 1 Reading Guide (Page 4)

Part IV: French and Indian War

A. Directions: Fill in the graphic organizer about the French and Indian War.

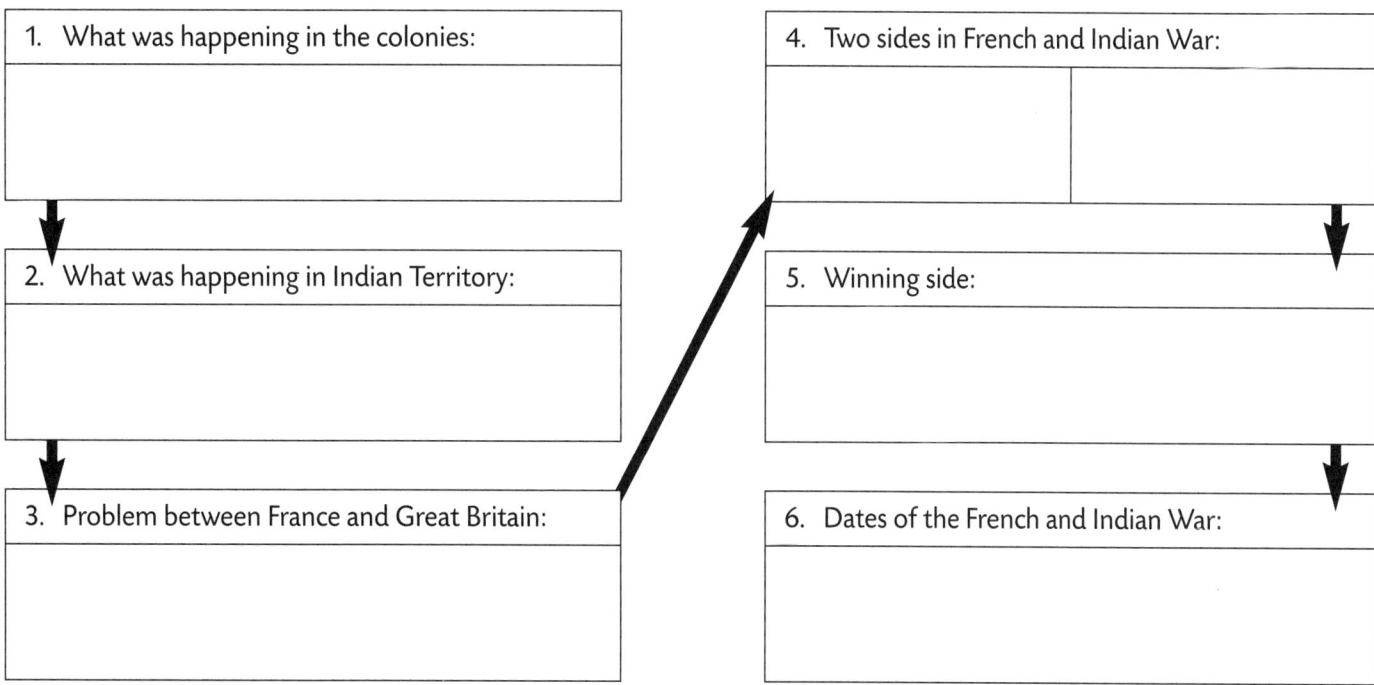

B. Directions: Determine the causes and effects of the French and Indian War by filling in the information.

Causes	Effects
1. Colonists kept expanding onto more land.	1.
2. The population continued to grow.	2.
3. Fights between Indians and settlers broke out.	3.
4. France lost colonies when the British won the war.	4.

© 2008 Gibbs Smith, Publisher
Accompanies *Tennessee Throught Time: The Later Years*

Name _____   Date _____

CHAPTER 2 ACTIVITY MASTER

Lesson 1 Reading Guide (Page 5)

Part V: American Independence

A. Directions: Answer the questions using complete sentences.

1. List three of the problems Great Britain faced after the French and Indian War.

   a. _____

   b. _____

   c. _____

2. Describe one **British** solution to one of the problems.
   _____

3. Describe one **colonist** solution to one of the problems.
   _____

B. Directions: Explain in your own words what Independence Day is to someone who has never heard of it. Tell **why** and **how** it is celebrated.

_____
_____
_____
_____
_____
_____
_____
_____

Name _____ Date _____

CHAPTER 2 ACTIVITY MASTER

Lesson 1 Reading Guide (Page 6)

Part VI: The American Revolution

A. Directions: Fill in the chart about the American Revolution.

	British	Colonists
Strengths		
Allies		
Occupation Before the War		
Results		

B. Directions: Write two ways that each picture on pp. 44-45 teaches you about the American Revolution.

Picture #1 (on the left)

1. _____
2. _____

Picture #2 (top right)

1. _____
2. _____

Picture #3 (bottom right)

1. _____
2. _____

Name _____   Date _____

CHAPTER 2 ACTIVITY MASTER

Lesson 1 Reading Guide (Page 7)

Part VII: A New Form of Government

A. Directions: Write the purpose of each document in the forms below.

B. Directions: Answer the questions with two or three sentences.

1. Why was the Bill of Rights added to the U.S. Constitution?

   _____
   _____
   _____

2. Why do we still base our government today on the U.S. Constitution?

   _____
   _____
   _____

3. If American citizens wanted to add something to the constitution, what could they do?

   _____
   _____
   _____

Name _____ Date _____

CHAPTER 2 ACTIVITY MASTER

Lesson 1 Reading Guide (Page 8)

Part VIII: Statehood for Tennessee

A. Directions: Read the following passage to answer the questions.

Preamble and Declaration of Rights

Whereas, The people of the territory of the United States south of the river Ohio, having the right of admission into the general government as a member state thereof, consistent with the Constitution of the United States, and the act of cession of the state of North Carolina, recognizing the ordinance for the government of the territory—of the United States north west of the Ohio River, by their delegates and representatives in convention assembled, did on the sixth day of February, in the year of our Lord one thousand seven hundred and ninety-six, ordain and establish a Constitution, or form of government, and mutually agreed with each other to form themselves into a free and independent state by the name of the state of Tennessee. . . .

1. What geographical details are given here about Tennessee?

2. What does the document seek admission into?

3. What does the word "cession" mean here?

4. What day did Tennessee establish a constitution?

5. What steps had to come before they formed "themselves into a free and independent state"?

6. What does this beginning part of the Tennessee State Constitution tell you about government?

© 2008 Gibbs Smith, Publisher
Accompanies *Tennessee Through Time: The Later Years*

Name _____   Date _____

CHAPTER 2 ACTIVITY MASTER

Lesson 1 Reading Guide (Page 9)

Part VIII: Statehood for Tennessee

B. Directions: Respond to the short answer questions.

1. What helped create the Territory South of the River Ohio?

2. Infer why the Southwest Territory grew so rapidly.

3. What requirements did the Southwest Territory meet to become a state?

4. How did Tennessee get its name?

5. Identify three facts about the date of Tennessee statehood.

Part IX: Memory Master

1. What was the largest Native American tribe in the Southeast?

2. What was the English colonists' war for independence called?

3. On what date did Tennessee become a state?

Part X: Note Home

Lesson 1 Reading Guide is a basic overview of what the students have learned in Chapter 2 pp. 34-49. The Memory Master questions are indicators of student comprehension. For supplemental activities, see experiencestatehistory.com and click on Tennessee. Check with the teacher for the student login password.

Name _____   Date _____

CHAPTER 2 ACTIVITY MASTER

Lesson 2 Reading Guide (Page 1)
Objective: 4.3.spi.5
Accompanies Student Edition pp. 50-53

Part I: Vocabulary

Directions: Fill in the blanks using the "Words to Understand" list from p. 50 in your textbook. Then write one paragraph on the lines below that uses all five Words to Understand. Give your paragraph a title.

    In 1. _____ North America, slavery was legal in 15 states, and they were all in the South. Across the nation, people were divided over the issue of slavery. More and more northern 2. _____ believed slavery was wrong. As the debates over the issue of slavery raged across the nation, southern leaders began talking about 3. _____. Southern states especially did not agree with Abraham Lincoln running for president, even though Lincoln said he would not 4. _____ slavery. But even without the support of the southern states, Lincoln won the presidential election. One by one, the southern states left the union and formed the 5. _____.

_____

_____
_____
_____
_____
_____
_____
_____
_____

Name _____ Date _____

CHAPTER 2 ACTIVITY MASTER

Lesson 2 Reading Guide (Page 2)

Part II: People to Know

Directions: Fill in the four square chart below about Jefferson Davis and Abraham Lincoln. Use your knowledge from the "Facts" boxes to help you make inferences. The first ones have been done to help you get started.

Abraham Lincoln	Jefferson Davis
Facts: Republican	**Facts:** Southern leader
Inferences: He was popular enough in the northern states to get elected.	**Inferences:** He was popular enough in the southern states to be chosen as president.

© 2008 Gibbs Smith, Publisher
Accompanies *Tennessee Throught Time: The Later Years*

Name _____ Date _____

CHAPTER 2 ACTIVITY MASTER

Lesson 2 Reading Guide (Page 3)

Part III: Places to Locate

Directions: On the map, locate and label the following places.

East Tennessee
Middle Tennessee
Pacific Ocean
Texas
West Tennessee

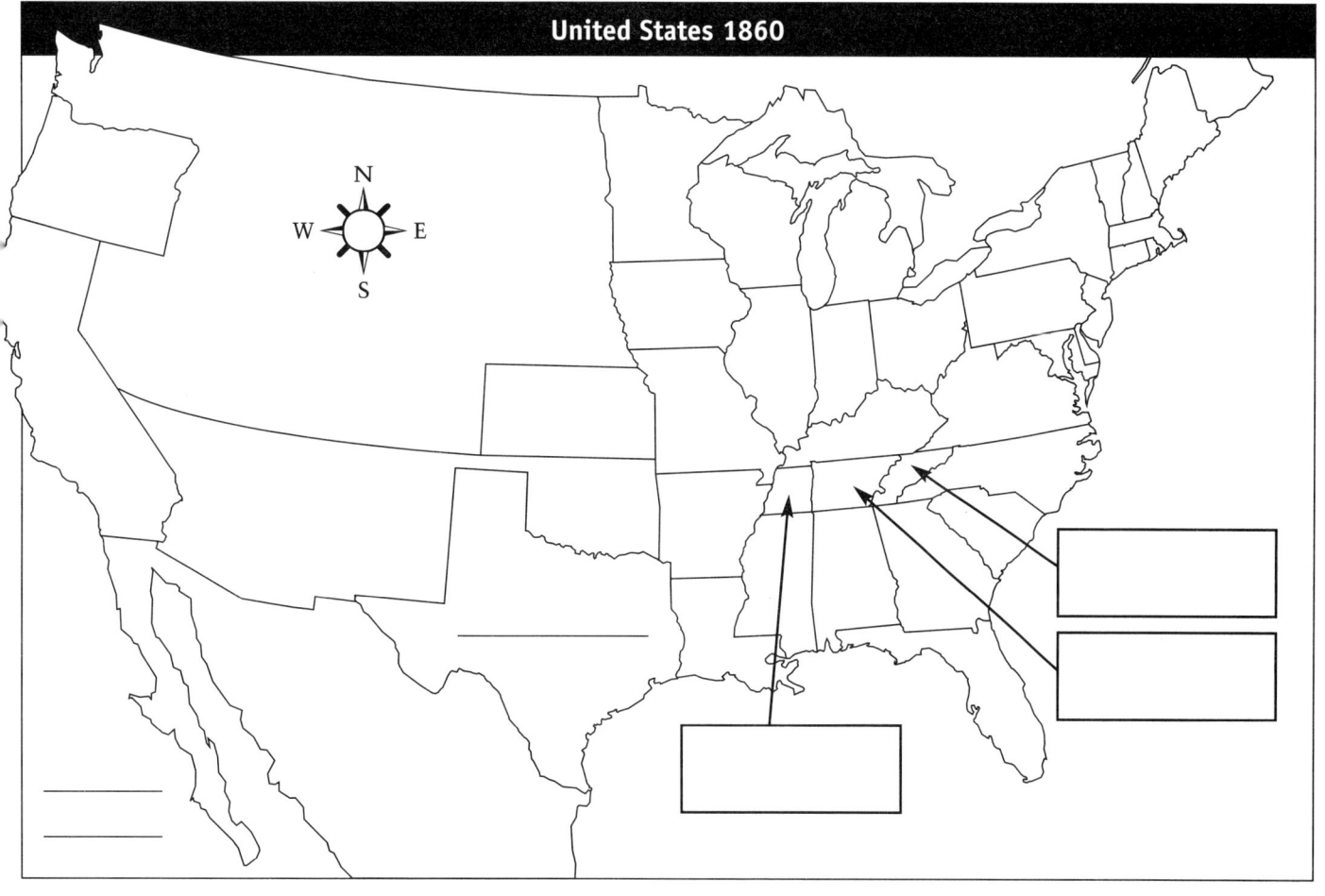

© 2008 Gibbs Smith, Publisher
Accompanies *Tennessee Throught Time: The Later Years*

Name _____ Date _____

CHAPTER 2 ACTIVITY MASTER

Lesson 2 Reading Guide (Page 4)

Part IV: Constructed Response

Directions: Answer the questions using critical thinking skills.

1. During the antebellum years, what were the economic differences between the North and the South?
   _____
   _____
   _____

2. Explain where Tennessee stood on the issue of slavery.
   _____
   _____
   _____

3. Describe the meaning of "states' rights."
   _____
   _____
   _____
   _____

Part V: Memory Master

1. What does "antebellum" mean?
   _____
   _____

2. What was the economy of the South based on before the Civil War?
   _____
   _____

3. What caused more debates after the Mexican War?
   _____
   _____

Part VI: Note Home

Lesson 2 Reading Guide is a basic overview of what the students have learned in Chapter 2 pp. 50-53. The Memory Master questions and the Constructed Response are indicators of student comprehension. For supplemental activities, see experiencestatehistory.com and click on Tennessee. Check with the teacher for the student login password.

Name _____   Date _____

CHAPTER 2 ACTIVITY MASTER

North and South

Objective: 5.5.spi.1
Accompanies Student Edition pp. 50-51

Directions: "What is, is," is an old saying. It means, "Just accept things as they are." Most people don't want to live like that, however. People always seem to be thinking about ways to make life better.

As you read this chapter, look for problems that the people tried to solve. Diagram the problems and one solution in the circles below. Then think of another way the people could have solved the problem.

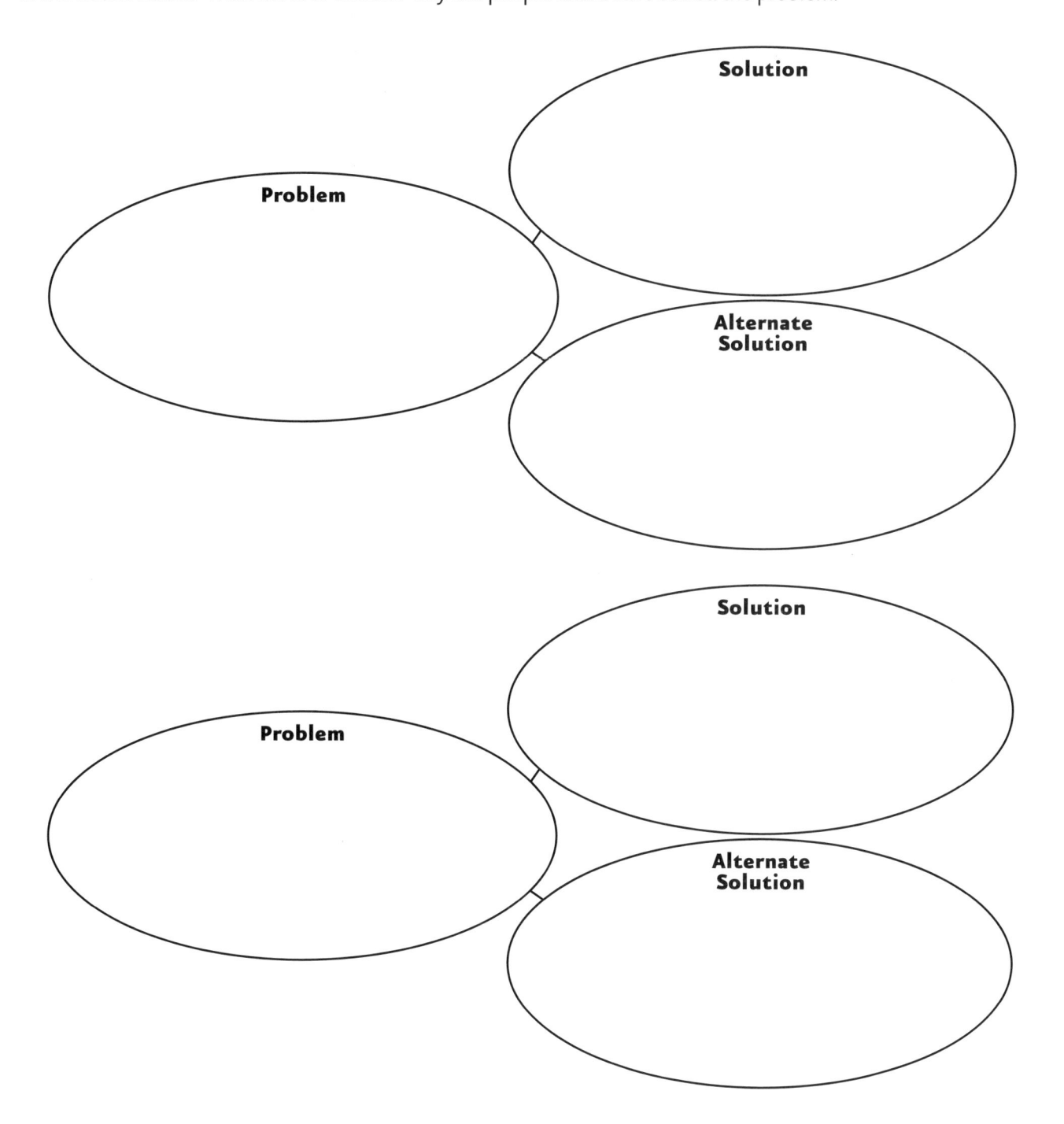

Problem

Solution

Alternate Solution

Problem

Solution

Alternate Solution

© 2008 Gibbs Smith, Publisher
Accompanies *Tennessee Throught Time: The Later Years*

33

Name _____ Date _____

CHAPTER 2 ACTIVITY MASTER

ELL Activity Master
Objectives: 5.1.spi.3, 5.6.spi.2
Accompanies Student Edition pp. 34-49

Directions: Write 10 main ideas from Chapter 2 in the boxes below.

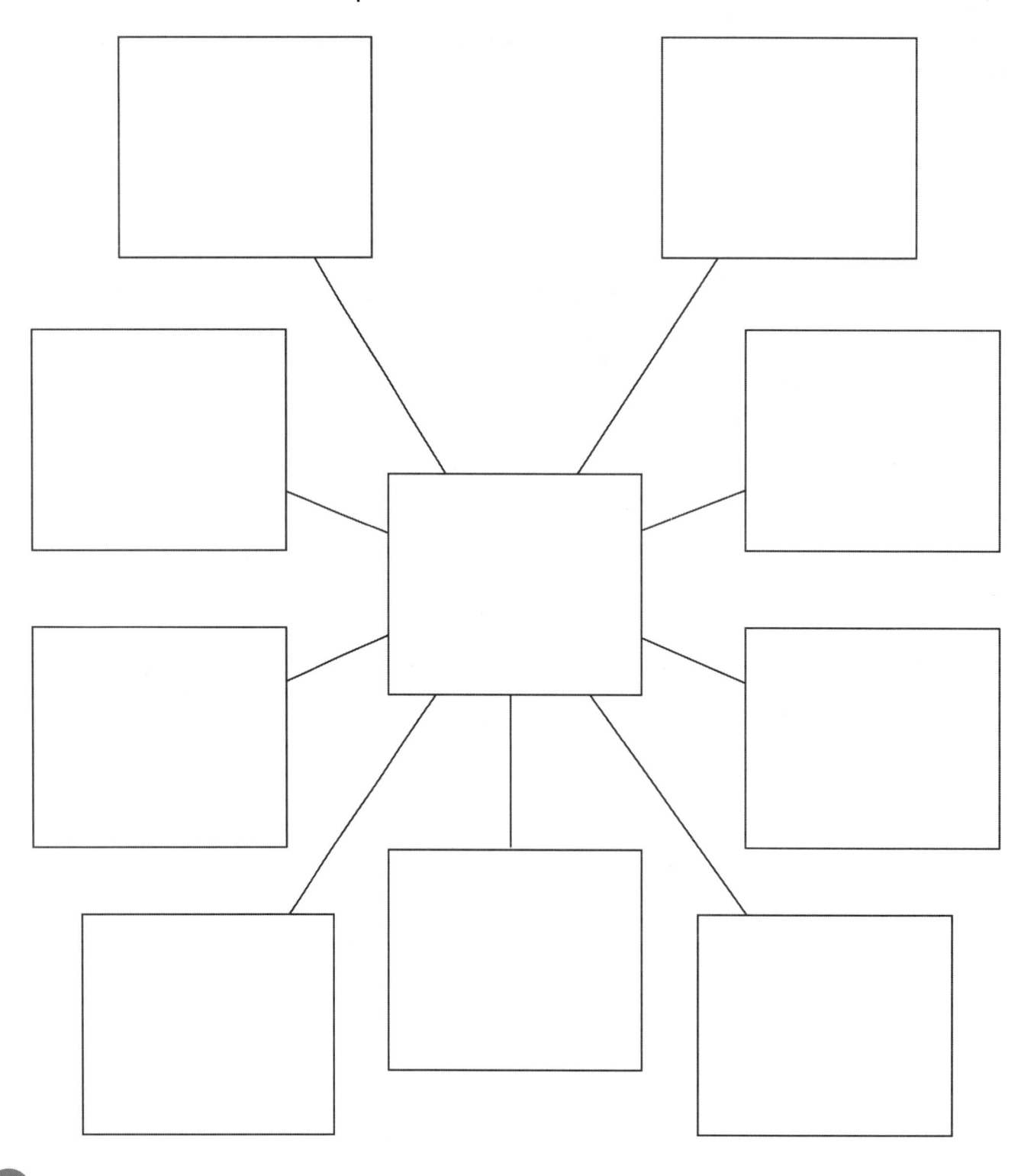

34

© 2008 Gibbs Smith, Publisher
Accompanies *Tennessee Throught Time: The Later Years*

Name _____ Date _____

CHAPTER 2 REVIEW

Chapter Review Study Guide (Page 1)

Objectives: 5.5.spi.1, 5.5.spi.2, 5.4.spi.5
Accompanies Student Edition pp. 32-55

Part I: Vocabulary

Directions: Study the following terms. You may also use your Lesson Reading Guides.

abolish
abolitionist
antebellum
Confederate States of America
secession

Part II: Constructed and Extended Response

Directions: Review the following ideas for constructed and extended response.

- What was the largest Native American tribe in the Southeast?
- What was the English colonists' war for independence called?
- On what date did Tennessee become a state?
- During the antebellum years, what were the economic differences between the North and the South?
- Explain where Tennessee stood on the issue of slavery.
- Describe the meaning of "states' rights."
- What does "antebellum" mean?
- What was the economy of the South based on before the Civil War?
- What caused more debates after the Mexican War?
- Why do you think the country was heading for war?

© 2008 Gibbs Smith, Publisher
Accompanies *Tennessee Through Time: The Later Years*

Name _____ Date _____

CHAPTER 2 REVIEW

Chapter Review Study Guide (Page 2)

Part III: Review

Directions: This chapter contains a review of Tennessee's beginnings up to the antebellum years. Summarize two main ideas from each of the sections below.

1. pp. 34-35 _____
   _____
   _____

2. pp. 36-37 _____
   _____
   _____

3. pp. 38-39 _____
   _____
   _____

4. pp. 40-41 _____
   _____
   _____

5. pp. 42-43 _____
   _____
   _____

6. pp. 44-45 _____
   _____
   _____

7. pp. 46-47 _____
   _____
   _____

8. pp. 48-49 _____
   _____
   _____

CHAPTER 3 TABLE OF CONTENTS

Chapter 3
The Civil War: A Nation and a State Divided (Student Edition pp. 56-99)

Table of Contents			
Activity Master	Standard Correlation	Page #	Accompanies Student Edition pages
Lesson 1 Reading Guide	5.5.spi.1, 5.5.spi.7, 5.6.spi.2	38-41	58-67
Lesson 2 Reading Guide	5.1.spi.2, 5.5.spi.2, 5.6.spi.2	42-44	68-83
Passport to History	5.5.spi.1	45	77
Battle of Shiloh	5.6.spi.2	46	76-77
Lesson 3 Reading Guide	5.1.spi.1, 5.1.spi.3, 5.5.spi.7, 5.6.spi.2	47-51	84-97
Gettysburg Address	5.5.spi.7	52	84-85
Civil War Surrender	5.5.spi.7	53	94
Civil War Survey	5.1.spi.3, 5.6.spi.2	54	97
ELL: Civil War People and Events	5.6.spi.2	55	58-97
Chapter Review	5.1.spi.1, 5.1.spi.2, 5.1.spi.3, 5.6.spi.2, 5.5.spi.7	56	56-99

© 2008 Gibbs Smith, Publisher
Accompanies *Tennessee Throught Time: The Later Years*

Name _____ Date _____

CHAPTER 3 ACTIVITY MASTER

Lesson 1 Reading Guide (Page 1)
Objectives: 5.5.spi.1, 5.5.spi.7, 5.6.spi.2
Accompanies Student Edition pp. 58-67

Part I: Vocabulary

Directions: Use the three vocabulary words from Lesson 1 to write a newspaper report on what was happening with the Southern states. Give your newspaper article a headline.

border states   civil war   secede

Name _____ Date _____

CHAPTER 3 ACTIVITY MASTER

Lesson 1 Reading Guide (Page 2)

Part II: People to Know

Directions: Next to the people listed, write one thing that person did during the Civil War.

1. Jefferson Davis _____

2. Isham Harris _____

3. Andrew Johnson _____

4. Abraham Lincoln _____

5. Northerners _____

6. Southerners _____

7. Marcus Woodcock _____

8. Felix Zollicoffer _____

Part III: Places to Locate

Directions: Next to each of the places, write more specific details about its location, including its state and what happened there.

1. Charleston Harbor: _____

2. Confederate States: _____

3. Fort Sumter: _____

4. Union States: _____

Name _____   Date _____

CHAPTER 3 ACTIVITY MASTER

Lesson 1 Reading Guide (Page 3)

Part IV: Short Answer

Directions: Answer the questions using your textbook.

1. Explain the tension that divided Tennessee. _____
_____

2. Describe what happened at the first Civil War battle. _____
_____

3. Identify the president of the Union and the president of the Confederacy. _____
_____

4. Explain Tennessee's final decision about secession. _____
_____

Part V: Memory Master

1. Who was the president of the Confederacy? _____
_____

2. Define "civil war." _____
_____

3. Tennessee was the _____ state to secede from the Union.

Part VI: Constructed Response

Directions: Answer the question using critical thinking skills.

What were two differences between the North's and the South's resources as the Civil War began?

_____
_____
_____
_____
_____
_____

Name _____   Date _____

CHAPTER 3 ACTIVITY MASTER

Lesson 1 Reading Guide (Page 4)

Part VII: Primary Source Reading

Directions: Read the account about the firing on Fort Sumter by Elizabeth Vanderville Darby recorded in 1940. Answer the questions that follow.

> Yes, I remember the firing on Fort Sumter, near Charleston, I was in my seventh year. General Beauregard had twice made a demand for its surrender, and the third time he told them that the 12th day of April would be the last day of grace. Everybody was solemn on that day, something like the expectancy of an impending total eclipse of sun, which I witnessed afterward in the late 90's. There was no playing on that day, but there [were] sad, anxious faces all around. News came that the fort had been fired on, and, soon afterward, war was declared. My father went out in Capt. Clingham's company, but he was soon transferred into the hospital service. He didn't face any bullets afterward, but he had to meet smallpox and diseases which carried away as many soldiers as grape shot.
>
> Source: http://memory.loc.gov/

1. Where do you think Elizabeth was during the firing on Fort Sumter? _____
_____

2. Why does she say that everyone was solemn on the 12th day of April? _____
_____

3. What news came after the fort had been fired on? _____
_____

4. What happened to Elizabeth's father? _____
_____

5. Why does Elizabeth talk about "grape shot"? _____
_____

Part VIII: Note Home

Lesson 1 Reading Guide is a basic overview of what the students have learned in Chapter 3 pp. 58-67. The Memory Master questions and the Constructed Response are indicators of student comprehension. For supplemental activities, see experiencestatehistory.com and click on Tennessee. Check with the teacher for the student login password.

Name _____   Date _____

CHAPTER 3 ACTIVITY MASTER

Lesson 2 Reading Guide (Page 1)
Objectives: 5.1.spi.2, 5.5.spi.2, 5.6.spi.2
Accompanies Student Edition pp. 68-83

Part I: Vocabulary

Directions: In each sentence, there is a vocabulary word that is used incorrectly. Underline the word, then write the correct word in the line provided at the end of the sentence.

1. Sam Watkins' writ of habeas corpus captured the glory, the defeat, the excitement, and the horror of the war. _____

2. After the Battle of Antietam, Abraham Lincoln issued a document known today as the Ku Klux Klan. _____

3. Union troops entered Nashville as the last Confederate soldiers in the city burned the strategist bridge across the Cumberland River. _____

4. Nathan Bedford Forrest became the Grand Wizard of the Emancipation Proclamation. _____

5. President Lincoln made an important decision to suspend the use of hardtack. _____

6. Nathan Bedford Forrest was a fast learner and a brilliant memoir. _____

7. Many soldiers had nothing to eat except a very hard cracker known as suspension. _____

Part II: People to Know

Directions: Next to each man's name, draw a symbol or small item that represents something from his life.

☐	Simon Buckner	☐	Robert E. Lee
☐	Frederick Douglass	☐	Abraham Lincoln
☐	Nathan Bedford Forrest	☐	Roger Taney
☐	Ulysses S. Grant	☐	Sam Watkins

© 2008 Gibbs Smith, Publisher
Accompanies *Tennessee Through Time: The Later Years*

Name _____   Date _____

CHAPTER 3 ACTIVITY MASTER

Lesson 2 Reading Guide (Page 2)

Part III: Places to Locate

Directions: Label the following locations on the map of Tennessee.

- Fort Donelson
- Fort Henry
- Fort Pillow
- Memphis
- Mississippi River
- Nashville
- Shiloh

Places to Locate in Tennessee

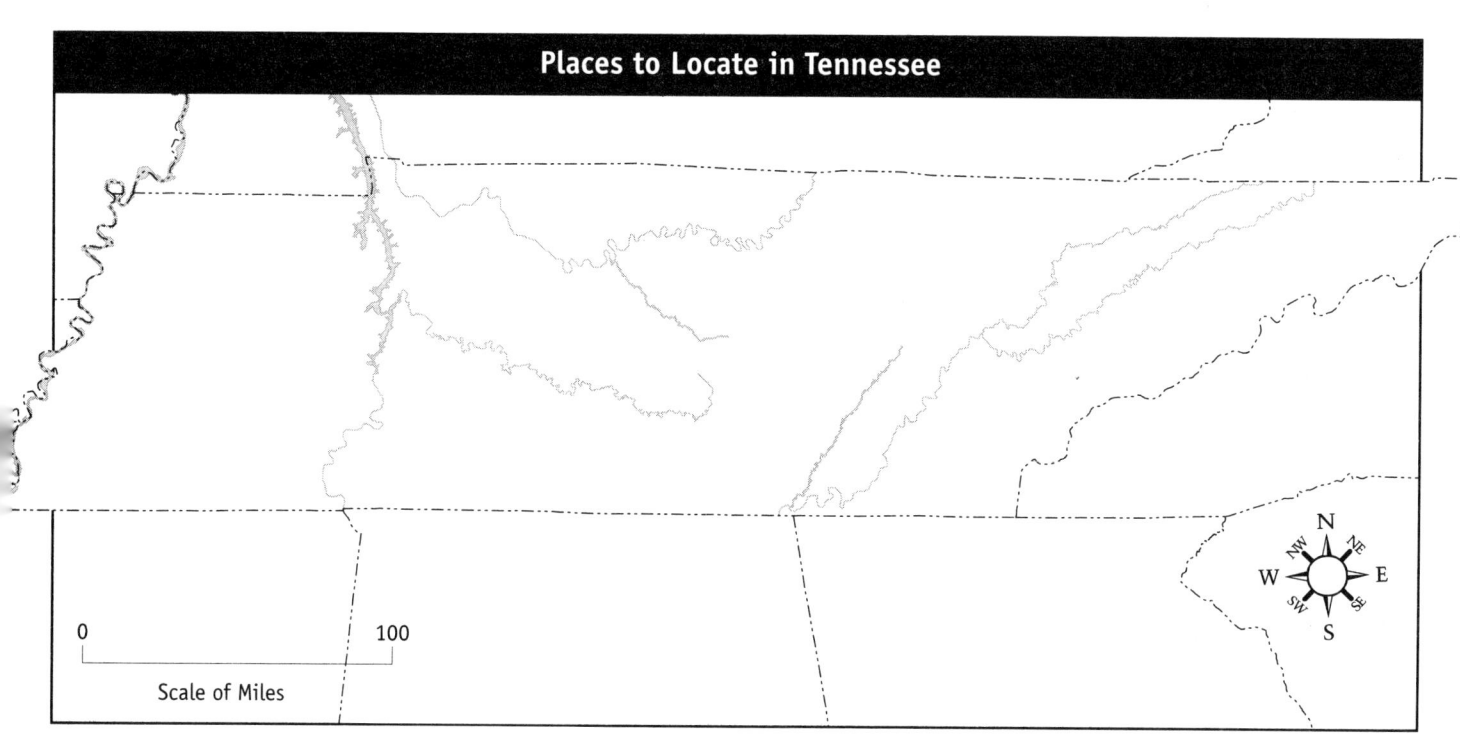

0 — 100
Scale of Miles

Part IV: Short Answer

Directions: Answer the questions using your textbook.

1. Describe the Anaconda Plan.
   _____
   _____

2. How was Tennessee an important site for Civil War battles?
   _____
   _____

3. Why did President Lincoln decide to suspend honoring writs of habeas corpus?
   _____
   _____

4. Identify how the Battle of Shiloh turned the war.
   _____
   _____

© 2008 Gibbs Smith, Publisher
Accompanies *Tennessee Through Time: The Later Years*

Name _____ Date _____

CHAPTER 3 ACTIVITY MASTER

Lesson 2 Reading Guide (Page 3)

Part V: Memory Master

1. What was the Anaconda Plan?
   _____
   _____

2. Why is Shiloh one of the most famous battles fought during the Civil War?
   _____
   _____

3. Name two accomplishments of Frederick Douglass.
   _____
   _____

Part VI: Constructed Response

Directions: Answer the question using critical thinking skills.

Why was the Emancipation Proclamation an important document? Why didn't it end the war?

_____
_____
_____
_____
_____
_____
_____
_____
_____

Part VII: Note Home

Lesson 2 Reading Guide is a basic overview of what the students have learned in Chapter 3 pp. 68-83. The Memory Master questions and the Constructed Response are indicators of student comprehension. For supplemental activities, see experiencestatehistory.com and click on Tennessee. Check with the teacher for the student login password.

Name _____   Date _____

CHAPTER 3 ACTIVITY MASTER

Passport to History

Objective: 5.5.spi.1
Accompanies Student Edition p. 77

PASSPORT TO HISTORY

Teacher Initial _____

Date _____

Directions: The excerpt from Samuel Watkins's book *Company Aytch* is reprinted here. Read it and mark it to help you answer the questions.

> On Sunday morning, the order was given for the whole army to advance, and to attack immediately. The fire opened—a ripping, roaring boom bang! . . . We [sneaked] through the woods, firing as we marched. The Yankee line was about two hundred yards off. In ten minutes, we were face to face with the foe.

1. Describe the writer. What were this person's duties during the Civil War?
   _____
   _____

2. Put yourself in this person's place. How would you feel if a battle took place in your hometown?
   _____
   _____

3. What would you do for protection?
   _____
   _____

4. What would you do to help others?
   _____
   _____

5. Since the Battle of Shiloh was a tragic event, why do you think we visit and remember the site today? What can we learn from it?
   _____
   _____

© 2008 Gibbs Smith, Publisher
Accompanies *Tennessee Through Time: The Later Years*

Name _____   Date _____

CHAPTER 3 ACTIVITY MASTER

Battle of Shiloh

Objective: 5.6.spi.2
Accompanies Student Edition pp. 76-77

Directions: Fill in the missing words and events from this timeline about the Battle of Shiloh.

1. The Union army entered _____.

2. The _____ headed south into Mississippi.

3. Union General Grant _____ to West Tennessee and set up camp at _____ _____.

4. Confederate General Johnston planned a _____ _____ on the Union forces at sunrise.

5. Confederate troops attacked _____ _____ who were eating breakfast.

6. _____ _____ was shot in the leg, and he bled to death.

7. The Union army was trapped against the _____ _____.

8. More Union soldiers arrived during the night from _____.

9. The _____ army pushed the _____ back and turned the tide of the battle.

10. Confederates retreated south into _____.

11. More than _____ men were injured or killed.

12. After _____, the _____ army controlled most of Middle and West Tennessee.

Name _____ Date _____

CHAPTER 3 ACTIVITY MASTER

Lesson 3 Reading Guide (Page 1)

Objectives: 5.1.spi.1, 5.1.spi.3, 5.5.spi.7, 5.6.spi.2
Accompanies Student Edition pp. 84-97

Part I: Vocabulary

Directions: For each vocabulary word, write three ideas from Lesson 3 that help you define and remember the word.

1. maritime

2. Reconstruction

© 2008 Gibbs Smith, Publisher
Accompanies *Tennessee Through Time: The Later Years*

Name _____ Date _____

CHAPTER 3 ACTIVITY MASTER

Lesson 3 Reading Guide (Page 2)

Part II: People to Know

Directions: Write how each person was involved in the Civil War. After each pair, write one thing the people had in common.

1. John Bell Hood: _____
   _____

2. Robert E. Lee: _____

   What they had in common: _____
   _____
   _____

3. Clara Barton: _____
   _____

4. Abraham Lincoln: _____

   What they had in common: _____
   _____
   _____

5. Ulysses S. Grant: _____
   _____

6. Andrew Johnson: _____

   What they had in common: _____
   _____
   _____

Name _____ Date _____

CHAPTER 3 ACTIVITY MASTER

Lesson 3 Reading Guide (Page 3)

Part IIIA: Places to Locate

Directions: In the space below, draw an outline of Tennessee from memory. Locate the following places. When you have finished, check your answers in the book on p. 95.

| Chattanooga | Chickamauga | Franklin | Nashville |

Part IIIB: Places to Locate

Directions: Write four reasons Gettysburg, Pennsylvania is a Civil War historic site.

1. _____
2. _____
3. _____
4. _____

Name _____   Date _____

CHAPTER 3 ACTIVITY MASTER

Lesson 3 Reading Guide (Page 4)

Part IV: Short Answer

Directions: Answer the questions in complete sentences.

1. Identify why the Battle of Gettysburg was a turning point in the Civil War.
   _____
   _____

2. How did Tennesseans help the war effort on the home front?
   _____
   _____

3. Identify two Civil War battles fought in Tennessee.
   _____
   _____

4. Explain how the Civil War ended.
   _____
   _____

Part V: Memory Master

1. Why do we remember Gettysburg today?
   _____
   _____

2. Why did the state of Tennessee have war destruction in every county?
   _____
   _____

3. What did Lincoln call his plan for rebuilding the nation after the Civil War?
   _____
   _____

Name _____   Date _____

CHAPTER 3 ACTIVITY MASTER

Lesson 3 Reading Guide (Page 5)

Part VI: Constructed Response

Directions: Answer the question using critical thinking skills.

In what ways did the Civil War affect Tennessee?

_____

_____

_____

_____

_____

_____

Part VII: Note Home

Lesson 3 Reading Guide is a basic overview of what the students have learned in Chapter 3 pp. 84-97. The Memory Master questions and the Constructed Response are indicators of student comprehension. For supplemental activities, see experiencestatehistory.com and click on Tennessee. Check with the teacher for the student login password.

Name _____ Date _____

CHAPTER 3 ACTIVITY MASTER

Gettysburg Address
Objective: 5.5.spi.7
Accompanies Student Edition pp. 84-85

Directions: Read the following draft of the Gettysburg Address. Answer the questions that follow.

Four score and seven years ago our fathers brought forth, upon this continent, a new nation, conceived in Liberty, and dedicated to the proposition that all men are created equal.

Now we are engaged in a great civil war, testing whether that nation, or any nation, so conceived, and so dedicated, can long endure. We are met here on a great battlefield of that war. We have come to dedicate a portion of it as a final resting place for those who here gave their lives that that nation might live. It is altogether fitting and proper that we should do this.

But in a larger sense we can not dedicate — we can not consecrate — we can not hallow this ground. The brave men, living and dead, who struggled, here, have consecrated it far above our poor power to add or detract. The world will little note, nor long remember, what we say here, but can never forget what they did here. It is for us, the living, rather to be dedicated here to the unfinished work which they have, thus far, so nobly carried on. It is rather for us to be here dedicated to the great task remaining before us — that from these honored dead we take increased devotion to that cause for which they here gave the last full measure of devotion — that we here highly resolve that these dead shall not have died in vain; that this nation shall have a new birth of freedom; and that this government of the people, by the people, for the people, shall not perish from the earth.

Source: http://www.loc.gov/exhibits/gadd/gatr2.html

1. A "score" is a time period of 20 years. What length of time does Lincoln name in the first line?

   _____

2. In the first paragraph, how does Lincoln describe the new nation created by "our fathers"?

   _____

3. In the second paragraph, what does Lincoln say we are testing?

   _____

4. Why does Lincoln say the ground cannot be dedicated or consecrated?

   _____

5. What is ironic about Lincoln saying, "The world will little note, nor long remember, what we say here . . ."?

   _____

6. How does Lincoln show respect for those who died at Gettysburg?

   _____

7. Describe the ending in your own words.

   _____

8. Why do you think people find this speech inspiring today?

   _____

Name _____   Date _____

CHAPTER 3 ACTIVITY MASTER

Civil War Surrender
Objective: 5.5.spi.7
Accompanies Student Edition p. 94

The Civil War ended when Confederate General Robert E. Lee surrendered (gave in) to Union General Ulysses S. Grant. Here are two passages that tell about the surrender. They are both primary sources, with one difference. The first one is by a man who lived during the war but did not see Lee meet with Grant. The second one is by a man who said he was in the room when Lee and Grant discussed the surrender.

Many years after the Civil War ended, Joshua Lawrence Chamberlain wrote down his memories of the war. He called his book *The Passing of the Armies.* Early on the morning of April 9, 1865, the Union army learned that General Lee of the Confederacy was surrendering. Chamberlain described it like this:

. . . we stood fast intensely waiting . . . I turned about, and there behind me, riding in between my two lines, appeared a commanding form, superbly mounted, . . . of imposing bearing, noble countenance, with expression of deep sadness overmastered by deeper strength. It is no other than Robert E. Lee!

Not long after, by another inleading road, appeared another form, plain, unassuming, simple, and familiar to our eyes . . . It is Grant! . . . sitting his saddle with the ease of a born master, taking no notice of anything, all his faculties gathered into intense thought and mighty calm. He seemed greater than I had ever seen him,—a look as if another world about him. No wonder I forgot altogether to salute him. Anything like that would have been too little.

This poem was written by an anonymous Confederate soldier. How does his point of view differ from Chamberlain's?

We were but a little band, standing there in the soft spring light of that Sabbath morn;
They were as the sands upon the sea shore, or as the leaves upon the forest trees...

Then rode down our lines that peer of Generals, Robert Edward Lee,
His head all bared and his noble face all clouded
With a sorrow deeper than tongue can tell or pen can paint
Is is a wonder then, that strong men, "men grown old in wars,"
Weep like children, and tearfully turning from, to them, the saddest sight on earth,
silently prepare to go back to their desolated homes?

Ah! Time, nor sorrow, nor no other grief, however great,
Can erase from memory's vellum* page the bitterness of that day.
(*paper made out of animal skin)

Do you think either source has bias? Give reasons why.

_____

_____

_____

_____

Name _____   Date _____

CHAPTER 3 ACTIVITY MASTER

Civil War Survey

Objectives: 5.1.spi.3, 5.6.spi.2
Accompanies Student Edition p. 97

Directions: Survey five people about the Civil War. Use the chart below to record their answers.

	What was the Civil War?	When was the Civil War?	Why was the Civil War fought?	Who won the Civil War?	What was the deadliest battle?	Where was the deadliest battle in Tennessee fought?	Name historic figures during the Civil War.
Person #1							
Person #2							
Person #3							
Person #4							
Person #5							

© 2008 Gibbs Smith, Publisher
Accompanies *Tennessee Through Time: The Later Years*

CHAPTER 3 ACTIVITY MASTER

ELL: Civil War People and Events
Objective: 5.6.spi.2
Accompanies Student Edition pp. 58-97

Part I: People
Directions: Write the matching letter in the blank next to each number.

___ 1. Jefferson Davis   A. surrendered the Confederate army in Virginia in 1865

___ 2. Frederick Douglass   B. founded the Red Cross

___ 3. Abraham Lincoln   C. said that all slaves in Southern states were free

___ 4. Ulysses S. Grant   D. fought for blacks to have equal rights

___ 5. Robert E. Lee   E. president of the Confederate States of America

___ 6. Clara Barton   F. Union general who accepted the Confederate surrender

Part II: Events
Directions: Write the matching letter in the blank next to each number.

___ 1. Southern secession   A. This was the North's plan to cut off supplies to the South.

___ 2. Battle at Fort Sumter   B. Southern states left the Union.

___ 3. Anaconda Plan   C. Confederates won this first battle of the Civil War.

___ 4. Emancipation Proclamation D. General Lee surrendered to General Grant on April 9, 1865.

___ 5. Battle of Shiloh   E. President Lincoln wrote a document to free all slaves.

___ 6. End of the Civil War   F. Union soldiers won this important battle in Tennessee.

Name _____   Date _____

CHAPTER 3 REVIEW

Chapter Review Study Guide (Page 1)
Objectives: 5.1.spi.1, 5.1.spi.2, 5.1.spi.3, 5.6.spi.2, 5.5.spi.7
Accompanies Student Text pp. 56-99

Part I: Vocabulary
Directions: Study the following terms. You may also use your Lesson Reading Guides.

border states	hardtack	suspension
civil war	Ku Klux Klan	writ of habeas corpus
secede	memoir	maritime
Emancipation Proclamation	strategist	Reconstruction

Part II: Review the following ideas for constructed and extended response.
- Who was the president of the Confederacy?
- Define "civil war."
- Tennessee was the _____ state to secede from the Union.
- What was the Anaconda Plan?
- Why is Shiloh one of the most famous battles fought during the Civil War?
- Name two accomplishments of Frederick Douglass.
- Why do we remember Gettysburg today?
- Why did the state of Tennessee have war destruction in every county?
- What did Lincoln call his plan for rebuilding the nation after the Civil War?
- What were two differences between the North's and the South's resources as the Civil War began?
- Why was the Emancipation Proclamation an important document? Why didn't it end the war?
- In what ways did the Civil War affect Tennessee?

Part III: Primary Source Reading
Read the following primary source account. Be able to discuss how the Civil War changed women's clothing styles.

> As the war went along, the matter of women and girls' dresses received much attention. There was no new cloth available. Old dresses were changed, sometimes turned wrong side out or remodeled. Grown folks' clothes were re-cut and fashioned into girl's dresses, dyed, and retrimmed. . . . Designs were nearly impossible; stripes predominated. Economy had to be observed and considered. Well, the styles then were long dresses with trails. . . . Women in those times wore shawls, each had an ambition to own and wear a cashmere shawl. They were lovely things, costly in material and beautiful in delicate embroideries. One of the everlasting griefs to the womanhood of the South was the searching for and taking away of these shawls when the Yankees made their other depredations in their march through the Confederacy.

Source: Oral history account by Elizabeth Vanderville Darby recorded in 1940 for the Federal Writers' Project from Library of Congress (http://memory.loc.gov/)

Chapter 4
Reconstruction and Beyond (Student Edition pp. 100-139)

Table of Contents			
Activity Master	Standard Correlation	Page #	Accompanies Student Edition pages
Lesson 1 Reading Guide	5.1.spi.2, 5.5.spi.3, 5.5.spi.7, 5.6.spi.3	58-60	102-113
Three Amendments	5.5.spi.7	61-62	109-110
Lesson 2 Reading Guide	5.1.spi.2, 5.2.spi.2, 5.2.spi.4, 5.5.spi.4, 5.5.spi.6	63-67	114-131
Passport to History	5.5.spi.7	68	121
Lesson 3 Reading Guide	5.1.spi.2, 5.5.spi.7, 5.6.spi.1	69-71	132-137
ELL: Reconstruction and Reform	5.1.spi.2, 5.5.spi.3	72	102-137
Chapter Review	5.1.spi.2, 5.2.spi.2, 5.2.spi.4, 5.5.spi.3, 5.5.spi.4, 5.5.spi.6, 5.6.spi.1	73-74	100-139

© 2008 Gibbs Smith, Publisher
Accompanies *Tennessee Through Time: The Later Years*

Name _____   Date _____

CHAPTER 4 ACTIVITY MASTER

Lesson 1 Reading Guide (Page 1)
Objectives: 5.1.spi.2, 5.5.spi.3, 5.5.spi.7, 5.6.spi.3
Accompanies Student Edition pp. 102-113

Part I: Vocabulary
Directions: Fill in the timeline with the correct vocabulary words.

amendment	epidemic	poll tax	sharecropping
barracks	freedmen	resign	steward
compromise	impeach	segregation	

1. The Tennessee General Assembly ratifies the Thirteenth _____.

2. Congress set up an agency to help former slaves, or _____.

3. Many former slaves who couldn't find jobs became _____, still working but not owning the land.

4. Fisk University, which was an army _____ during the Civil War, opened in Nashville.

5. Many Republicans were angry about Andrew Johnson's plans for Reconstruction, so they voted to _____ him.

6. In the 1870s, three yellow fever _____ hit Memphis, and thousands of people died.

7. Robert R. Church Sr., the South's first African American millionaire, first worked as a cabin boy and then a _____.

8. Governor Brownlow made some people happy when he _____ to become a U.S. senator.

9. The new Tennessee constitution called for a _____ for citizens to pay before they could vote.

10. The _____ law separated people by race so that within 15 years, there were no black members left in the Tennessee General Assembly.

11. The presidential election of 1876 had to be settled by a _____.

Name _____ Date _____

CHAPTER 4 ACTIVITY MASTER

Lesson 1 Reading Guide (Page 2)

Part II: People to Know

Directions: Using the names in the word bank, group the "People to Know" under the category where he fits best.

John Wilkes Booth	Rutherford B. Hayes	Robert Taylor
William Brownlow	Abraham Lincoln	Samuel J. Tilden
Robert R. Church Sr.	Dewitt Senter	
Clinton B. Fisk	Alfred Taylor	

Tennessee Governor	U.S. Presidential Candidate	Millionaire	Assassin	University Name

Directions: Now choose two names and write a connection between them.

_____

_____

© 2008 Gibbs Smith, Publisher
Accompanies *Tennessee Through Time: The Later Years*

Name _____ Date _____

CHAPTER 4 ACTIVITY MASTER

Lesson 1 Reading Guide (Page 3)

Part III: Short Answer

Directions: Answer the questions using complete sentences.

1. Describe Andrew Johnson's plan for Reconstruction.
   _____
   _____

2. What three new amendments were ratified?
   _____
   _____

3. Explain what happened during the Violent Reconstruction.
   _____
   _____

4. Identify one reason that progress was needed to improve the lives of African Americans.
   _____
   _____

Part IV: Memory Master

1. What was the goal of Reconstruction?
   _____
   _____

2. What hardships did sharecroppers face?
   _____
   _____

3. Even though the Fourteenth Amendment gave voting rights to blacks, they were still prevented from voting. How?
   _____
   _____

Part V: Constructed Response

Directions: Answer the question using critical thinking skills.

How was life both better and worse for African Americans during Reconstruction?
_____
_____

Part VI: Note Home

Lesson 1 Reading Guide is a basic overview of what the students have learned in Chapter 4 pp. 102-113. The Memory Master questions and the Constructed Response are indicators of student comprehension. For supplemental activities, see experiencestatehistory.com and click on Tennessee. Check with the teacher for the student login password.

Name _____ Date _____

CHAPTER 4 ACTIVITY MASTER

Three Amendments (Page 1)
Objective: 5.5.spi.7
Accompanies Student Edition pp. 109-110

Directions: Read each amendment from the U.S. Constitution. Answer the questions that follow.

Thirteenth Amendment

Section 1. Neither slavery nor involuntary servitude, except as a punishment for crime whereof the party shall have been duly convicted, shall exist within the United States, or any place subject to their jurisdiction.

Section 2. Congress shall have power to enforce this article by appropriate legislation.

1. What is "involuntary servitude"? _____

2. Where is slavery not allowed to exist? _____

3. Rewrite this amendment in your own words. _____

4. How did this amendment change life in America? _____

Fourteenth Amendment

Section 1. All persons born or naturalized in the United States, and subject to the jurisdiction thereof, are citizens of the United States and of the State wherein they reside. No State shall make or enforce any law which shall abridge the privileges or immunities of citizens of the United States; nor shall any State deprive any person of life, liberty, or property, without due process of law; nor deny to any person within its jurisdiction the equal protection of the laws.

5. Who is said to be a citizen of the United States? _____

6. What does "abridge the privileges or immunities of citizens" mean? _____

7. Rewrite this amendment in your own words. _____

8. How did this amendment change life for African Americans? _____

© 2008 Gibbs Smith, Publisher
Accompanies *Tennessee Through Time: The Later Years*

Name _____ Date _____

CHAPTER 4 ACTIVITY MASTER

Three Amendments (Page 2)

> **Fifteenth Amendment**
>
> Section 1. The right of citizens of the United States to vote shall not be denied or abridged by the United States or by any State on account of race, color, or previous condition of servitude.

9. Does the word "abridged" here mean the same as it did in the Fourteenth Amendment? Why or why not?

10. What does "previous condition of servitude" mean? _____

11. Rewrite this amendment in your own words. _____

12. How did this amendment change life for all Americans? _____

13. Why do you think Southern states were required to ratify these three amendments to re-enter the Union?

14. Why did some citizens choose to ignore these amendments? _____

Name _____ Date _____

CHAPTER 4 ACTIVITY MASTER

Lesson 2 Reading Guide (Page 1)

Objectives: 5.1.spi.2, 5.2.spi.2, 5.2.spi.4, 5.5.spi.4, 5.5.spi.6
Accompanies Student Edition pp. 114-131

Part I: Vocabulary

Directions: Define each word. Then write a heading for each group of words.

Group 1 Heading: _____

1. American Federation of Labor _____

2. labor union _____

3. laborer _____

4. strike _____

5. strikebreaker _____

6. surplus _____

Group 2 Heading: _____

7. investors _____

8. stock _____

9. corporation _____

Name _____   Date _____

CHAPTER 4 ACTIVITY MASTER

Lesson 2 Reading Guide (Page 2)

Group 3 Heading: _____

10. boom _____

11. carpetbagger _____

12. urbanization _____

13. suburb _____

Group 4 Heading: _____

14. homesteader _____

15. isolated _____

16. sod _____

Group 5 Heading: _____

17. famine _____

18. transcontinental _____

19. immigrants _____

Name _____ Date _____

CHAPTER 4 ACTIVITY MASTER

Lesson 2 Reading Guide (Page 3)

Part II: People to Know

Directions: Write two facts about each person. Then write one sentence describing how that person is different from the others in Lesson 2.

1. Thomas Edison: _____
   _____
   _____

2. Samuel Gompers: _____
   _____
   _____

3. Emma Lazarus: _____
   _____
   _____

4. Benjamin Thomas: _____
   _____
   _____

5. Joseph Whitehead: _____
   _____
   _____

Name _____ Date _____

CHAPTER 4 ACTIVITY MASTER

Lesson 2 Reading Guide (Page 4)

Part III: Places to Locate

Directions: On the map, locate and label the following locations.

Chattanooga
Great Plains
Great Smoky Mountains National Park
New York City, New York

Name _____   Date _____

CHAPTER 4 ACTIVITY MASTER

Lesson 2 Reading Guide (Page 5)

Part IV: Short Answer

Directions: Answer the questions using complete sentences.

1. What caused urbanization in Tennessee?
   _____
   _____

2. How did railroads and immigrants change the economy?
   _____
   _____

3. What were some of the challenges homesteaders faced on the Great Plains?
   _____
   _____

4. What did labor unions fight for?
   _____
   _____

Part V: Memory Master

1. Why was there an economic boom after the Civil War?
   _____

2. Why did settlers on the Great Plains give up and move?
   _____

3. What was the goal of labor unions?
   _____

Part VI: Constructed Response

Directions: Answer the question using critical thinking skills.

What were two of the changes that occurred in the economy of the New South?
_____
_____

Part VII: Note Home

Lesson 2 Reading Guide is a basic overview of what the students have learned in Chapter 4 pp. 114-131. The Memory Master questions and the Constructed Response are indicators of student comprehension. For supplemental activities, see experiencestatehistory.com and click on Tennessee. Check with the teacher for the student login password.

© 2008 Gibbs Smith, Publisher
Accompanies *Tennessee Through Time: The Later Years*

Name _____   Date _____

CHAPTER 4 ACTIVITY MASTER

Passport to History
Objective: 5.5.spi.7
Accompanies Student Edition p. 121

The New Colossus
Give me your tired, your poor
Your huddled masses yearning to breathe free
The wretched refuse of your teeming shore
Send these the homeless tempest-tossed to me
I lift my lamp beside the golden door!

1. What words does Lazarus use to describe people who come to America?
   _____
   _____

2. Why would people coming to America be "yearning to breathe free"?
   _____
   _____

3. What does Lazarus mean by "I lift my lamp beside the golden door"?
   _____
   _____

4. If you were thinking of immigrating to America, would this poem help you feel welcome here? Why or why not?
   _____
   _____

Use the space below to create an illustration to go along with Lazarus's poem.

Name _____ Date _____

CHAPTER 4 ACTIVITY MASTER

Lesson 3 Reading Guide (Page 1)
Objectives: 5.1.spi.2, 5.5.spi.7, 5.6.spi.1
Accompanies Student Edition pp. 132-137

Part I: Vocabulary
Directions: For each vocabulary word, write two different sentences. The first sentence should use the word as it is used in this chapter. The second sentence should use the word as it is used in today's time.

1. exposition _____
   _____
   _____

2. illiteracy _____
   _____
   _____

3. Prohibition _____
   _____
   _____

4. reform _____
   _____
   _____

5. replica _____
   _____
   _____

6. revival _____
   _____
   _____

7. segregate _____
   _____
   _____

© 2008 Gibbs Smith, Publisher
Accompanies *Tennessee Through Time: The Later Years*

Name _____   Date _____

CHAPTER 4 ACTIVITY MASTER

Lesson 3 Reading Guide (Page 2)

Part II: People to Know

Directions: Write three facts about each person on the chart.

Sam Jones	Lide Smith Meriwether	Tom Ryman	Ida B. Wells-Barnett

Part III: Places to Locate

Directions: Locate and label the following locations on the world map.

Athens, Greece	Cuba	Nashville	Philippines	Puerto Rico

© 2008 Gibbs Smith, Publisher
Accompanies *Tennessee Through Time: The Later Years*

Name _____ Date _____

CHAPTER 4 ACTIVITY MASTER

Lesson 3 Reading Guide (Page 3)

Part IV: Short Answer

Directions: Answer the questions using complete sentences.

1. What was the women's movement spreading across the South?
   _____
   _____

2. What was the Centennial Exposition?
   _____
   _____

3. Describe one area of progress as the 19th century ended.
   _____
   _____

Part V: Memory Master

1. What was Prohibition?
   _____

2. Why didn't more money provide better results for education?
   _____

3. What did Ida Wells write about and work for?
   _____

Part VI: Constructed Response

Directions: Answer the question using critical thinking skills.

What do women's rights, Prohibition, education, and African Americans have in common at the end of the century?
_____
_____

Part VII: Note Home

Lesson 3 Reading Guide is a basic overview of what the students have learned in Chapter 4 pp. 132-137. The Memory Master questions and the Constructed Response are indicators of student comprehension. For supplemental activities, see experiencestatehistory.com and click on Tennessee. Check with the teacher for the student login password.

© 2008 Gibbs Smith, Publisher
Accompanies *Tennessee Through Time: The Later Years*

Name _____   Date _____

CHAPTER 4 ACTIVITY MASTER

ELL: Reconstruction and Reform
Objectives: 5.1.spi.2, 5.5.spi.3
Accompanies Student Edition pp. 102-137

Part I: Definitions
Directions: Write the correct word to fit the definition. Understand the major parts of Reconstruction and reform at the end of the 1800s.

Reconstruction   reform

1. _____ changes made in order to improve something
2. _____ the time in U.S. history when the South needed to be rebuilt after the Civil War

Part II: Chart
Directions: Fill in the chart.

Johnson's Reconstruction	End of Reconstruction	Reform
1. At first, Andrew Johnson wanted to _____ the Confederate leaders.	5. Federal soldiers remained in the South for more than _____ years.	9. Labor unions fought for _____ working conditions and higher _____.
2. Later he suggested the Confederate states be returned to the Union as soon as they approved the _____.	6. In the presidential election of 1876, Democrat _____ _____ ran against Republican _____.	10. Women formed _____ organizations to fight for the right to _____.
3. Congress disagreed with Johnson and decided to _____ him.	7. When the votes were counted, both parties claimed to _____.	11. Because Tennessee's _____ was increasing, _____ needed reform.
4. Congress passed a law that Confederate states could return to the Union if they approved both the _____ and _____.	8. A _____ was agreed upon that allowed Hayes to become president if he removed all _____ _____ from the South.	12. Ida B. Wells was one reformist who fought for _____ _____ for African Americans.

72

© 2008 Gibbs Smith, Publisher
Accompanies *Tennessee Through Time: The Later Years*

Name _____   Date _____

CHAPTER 4 REVIEW

Chapter Review Study Guide (Page 1)
Objectives: 5.1.spi.2, 5.2.spi.2, 5.2.spi.4, 5.5.spi.3, 5.5.spi.4, 5.5.spi.6, 5.6.spi.1
Accompanies Student Text pp. 100-139

Part I: Vocabulary
Directions: Study the following terms. You may also use your Lesson Reading Guides.

amendment	segregation	strike	urbanization	exposition
barracks	sharecropping	strikebreaker	suburb	illiteracy
compromise	steward	surplus	homesteader	Prohibition
epidemic	American	investors	isolated	reform
freedmen	Federation of	stock	sod	replica
impeach	Labor	corporation	famine	revival
poll tax	labor union	boom	transcontinental	segregate
resign	laborer	carpetbagger	immigrants	

Part II: Review the following ideas for constructed and extended response.
- Describe Andrew Johnson's plan for Reconstruction.
- What three new amendments were ratified?
- Explain what happened during the Violent Reconstruction.
- How did Reconstruction end?
- What was the goal of Reconstruction?
- What hardships did sharecroppers face?
- Even though the Fourteenth Amendment gave voting rights to blacks, they were still prevented from voting. How?
- How was life both better and worse for African Americans during Reconstruction?
- What was the goal of Reconstruction?
- What hardships did sharecroppers face?
- Review the Thirteenth, Fourteenth, and Fifteenth Amendments.
- What caused urbanization in Tennessee?
- How did railroads and immigrants change the economy?
- What were some of the challenges homesteaders faced on the Great Plains?
- What did labor unions fight for?
- Why was there an economic boom after the Civil War?
- Why did settlers on the Great Plains give up and move?
- What was the goal of labor unions?
- What were two of the changes that occurred in the economy of the New South?
- What was the women's movement spreading across the South?
- What was the Centennial Exposition?
- Describe one area of progress as the 19th century ended.
- What was Prohibition?
- Why didn't more money provide better results for education?
- What did Ida Wells write about and work for?
- What did women's rights, Prohibition, education, and African Americans have in common at the end of the century?

© 2008 Gibbs Smith, Publisher
Accompanies *Tennessee Throught Time: The Later Years*

Name _____ Date _____

CHAPTER 4 REVIEW

Chapter Review Study Guide (Page 2)

Part III: Review

Use the space below to draw one image from each lesson in Chapter 4.

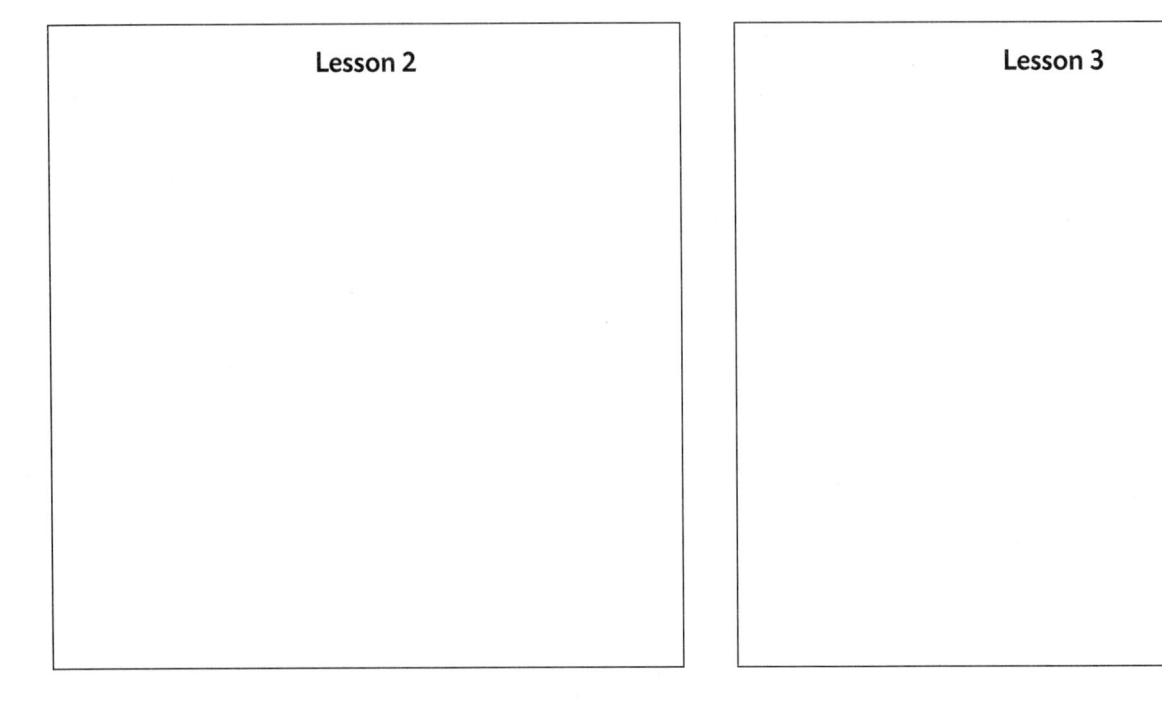

Lesson 1

Lesson 2

Lesson 3

Chapter 5
The Dawn of a New Century (Student Edition pp. 104-179)

Table of Contents			
Activity Master	Standard Correlation	Page #	Accompanies Student Edition pages
Lesson 1 Reading Guide	5.1.spi.1, 5.1.spi.2, 5.6.spi.1, 5.6.spi.3	76-79	142-159
Passport to History	5.1.spi.1	80	145
Lesson 2 Reading Guide	5.1.spi.1, 5.1.spi.2, 5.1.spi.3, 5.4.spi.5, 5.5.spi.7, 5.6.spi.2	81-83	160-169
World War I	5.5.spi.7	84-87	161-165
League of Nations	5.5.spi.7	88-89	169
Lesson 3 Reading Guide	5.1.spi.2, 5.4.spi.2, 5.4.spi.3, 5.6.spi.1, 5.6.spi.3	90-91	170-177
ELL: Problem-Solution Frame	5.6.spi.3	92	142-177
Chapter Review	5.1.spi.1, 5.1.spi.2, 5.1.spi.3, 5.4.spi.3, 5.5.spi.7, 5.6.spi.1, 5.6.spi.2	93	140-179

Name _____ Date _____

CHAPTER 5 ACTIVITY MASTER

Lesson 1 Reading Guide (Page 1)
Objectives: 5.1.spi.1, 5.1.spi.2, 5.6.spi.1, 5.6.spi.3
Accompanies Student Edition pp. 142-159

Part I: Vocabulary

Directions: Each vocabulary word here is spelled incorrectly. Correct the spelling, and write the definition next to each word.

1. boycot: _____

2. concervation: _____

3. coruption: _____

4. distellery: _____

5. edittorial: _____

6. industrialzation: _____

7. Jim Crowe laws: _____

8. laber laws: _____

9. pardun: _____

10. seamstres: _____

11. settlment house: _____

12. stochyard: _____

13. textyle: _____

14. utilitiy: _____

Name _____ Date _____

CHAPTER 5 ACTIVITY MASTER

Lesson 1 Reading Guide (Page 2)

Part II: People to Know

Directions: Using the names in the word bank, group these "People to Know" under the Progressive category where he/she fits best. Then choose one figure you admire and write four sentences about him/her.

Jane Addams	Lizzie Crozier French	Sallie Hill Sawyer
Edward Ward Carmack	Elizabeth Avery Meriwether	William Seward
Jasper Newton "Jack" Daniel	Randolph Miller	Emma Rochelle Wheeler
Henry Ford	Theodore Roosevelt	

Expansion	Conservation	Cities	Transportation

Prohibition	African Americans	Women

The person I chose is _____.

_____
_____
_____
_____

© 2008 Gibbs Smith, Publisher
Accompanies *Tennessee Through Time: The Later Years*

Name _____   Date _____

CHAPTER 5 ACTIVITY MASTER

Lesson 1 Reading Guide (Page 3)

Part III: Places to Locate

Directions: Write two sentences to describe the relative and absolute locations of the following locations:

1. Alaska _____
   _____

2. Hawaii _____
   _____

3. Panama Canal _____
   _____

4. What do these three locations have geographically in common? _____
   _____

Part IV: Short Answer

Directions: Answer the questions using your textbook.

1. Define the Progressive Era.
   _____
   _____

2. What progress was made for women's rights?
   _____
   _____

3. Explain how automobiles affected U.S. culture.
   _____
   _____

4. Identify one reason that progress was needed to improve the lives of African Americans.
   _____
   _____

Name _____ Date _____

CHAPTER 5 ACTIVITY MASTER

Lesson 1 Reading Guide (Page 4)

Part V: Memory Master

1. Name three things people wanted to reform during the Progressive Era.
   _____
   _____

2. Explain how the terms "wet" and "dry" connect to Prohibition.
   _____
   _____

3. What were Jim Crow laws?
   _____
   _____

Part VI: Constructed Response

Directions: Answer the question using critical thinking skills.

How did industrialization inspire progressive changes?
_____
_____

Part VII: Note Home

Lesson 1 Reading Guide is a basic overview of what the students have learned in Chapter 5 pp. 142-159. The Memory Master questions and the Constructed Response are indicators of student comprehension. For supplemental activities, see experiencestatehistory.com and click on Tennessee. Check with the teacher for the student login password.

© 2008 Gibbs Smith, Publisher
Accompanies *Tennessee Through Time: The Later Years*

Name _____ Date _____

CHAPTER 5 ACTIVITY MASTER

Passport to History

Objective: 5.1.spi.1
Accompanies Student Edition p. 145

PASSPORT TO HISTORY

Teacher Initial _____
Date _____

Directions: In the first column, record why any three things have changed over the last 100 years. In the second column, write three questions you would ask someone in 1901. In the third column make three predictions for things that will change in the next 100 years. When you are finished, turn your chart in for a stamp in your passport.

Changes Over the Last 100 Years	Questions for Someone in 1901	Predictions for the Next 100 Years
1.	1.	1.
2.	2.	2.
3.	3.	3.

© 2008 Gibbs Smith, Publisher
Accompanies *Tennessee Through Time: The Later Years*

Name _____ Date _____

CHAPTER 5 ACTIVITY MASTER

Lesson 2 Reading Guide (Page 1)

Objectives: 5.1.spi.1, 5.1.spi.2, 5.1.spi.3, 5.4.spi.5, 5.5.spi.7, 5.6.spi.2
Accompanies Student Edition pp. 160-169

Part I: Vocabulary

Directions: Write a sentence for each vocabulary word that *also* includes the term "United States."

1. alliance _____
_____

2. draft _____
_____

3. neutral _____
_____

4. submarine _____
_____

5. truce _____
_____

6. armistice _____
_____

7. veterans _____
_____

Part II: People to Know

Directions: Read the following clues to determine which person fits the description.

| Herbert Hoover | Lawrence D. Tyson | Alvin C. York |
| Charles McGhee Tyson | Woodrow Wilson | |

1. _____ I wanted World War I to be the last war ever fought. I knew that if the world was organized into the League of Nations that international peace would be established.
2. _____ I had a duty to fight in a war that contradicted my religious beliefs. Though I did not believe in fighting, I knew I could help, and I assisted in capturing 132 German soldiers.
3. _____ I found out that my son's military plane had been shot down over the North Atlantic, so I sailed out to find his body. After the war, I served in the United States Senate.
4. _____ I was in charge of the Food Administration, and I believed that "food [would] win the war." I organized days like "Meatless Mondays" to be able to send more food overseas.
5. _____ I joined the navy to become a pilot. I got shot down by the Germans. Today there is a Tennessee airport named after me.

© 2008 Gibbs Smith, Publisher
Accompanies *Tennessee Through Time: The Later Years*

Name _____ Date _____

CHAPTER 5 ACTIVITY MASTER

Lesson 2 Reading Guide (Page 2)

Part III: Places to Locate

Directions: On the map, locate and label the following countries.

Austria-Hungary	Germany	Russia	Turkey
France	Great Britain	Serbia	

Name _____ Date _____

CHAPTER 5 ACTIVITY MASTER

Lesson 2 Reading Guide (Page 3)

Part IV: Short Answer

Directions: Answer the questions using your textbook.

1. What started World War I?
   _____
   _____

2. Identify one reason the United States wanted to stay neutral.
   _____
   _____

3. Why was World War I called a "modern war"?
   _____
   _____

4. How did Americans help in the war effort?
   _____
   _____
   _____

Part V: Memory Master

1. Identify the new underwater invention the Germans used in World War I.
   _____

2. How did Tennesseans help in the war effort?
   _____

3. Why did Woodrow Wilson want to form the League of Nations?
   _____

Part VI: Constructed Response

Directions: Describe President Wilson's plan for world peace. Did it succeed?
_____
_____

Part VII: Note Home

Lesson 2 Reading Guide is a basic overview of what the students have learned in Chapter 5 pp. 160-169. The Memory Master questions and the Constructed Response are indicators of student comprehension. For supplemental activities, see experiencestatehistory.com and click on Tennessee. Check with the teacher for the student login password.

© 2008 Gibbs Smith, Publisher
Accompanies *Tennessee Through Time: The Later Years*

World War I (Page 1)

Objective: 5.5.spi.7
Accompanies Student Edition pp. 161-165

Directions: Read the following speech given by President Woodrow Wilson to the joint houses of Congress on April 2, 1917. Wilson here outlines the case for declaring war upon Germany. Four days later, a formal declaration of war was issued. After you read the speech, answer the questions that follow. The paragraphs are numbered and used as references in the questions.

1. I have called the Congress into extraordinary session because there are serious, very serious, choices of policy to be made, and made immediately, which it was neither right nor constitutionally permissible that I should assume the responsibility of making.

2. On the third of February last I officially laid before you the extraordinary announcement of the Imperial German Government that on and after the first day of February it was its purpose to put aside all restraints of law or of humanity and use its submarines to sink every vessel that sought to approach either the ports of Great Britain and Ireland or the western coasts of Europe or any of the ports controlled by the enemies of Germany within the Mediterranean. . . .

3. Even hospital ships and ships carrying relief to the sorely bereaved and stricken people of Belgium, though the latter were provided with safe conduct through the proscribed areas by the German Government itself and were distinguished by unmistakable marks of identity, have been sunk with the same reckless lack of compassion or of principle. . . .

4. I was for a little while unable to believe that such things would in fact be done by any government that had hitherto subscribed to the humane practices of civilized nations. International law had its origin in the attempt to set up some law which would be respected and observed upon the seas, where no nation had right of dominion and where lay the free highways of the world.

5. I am not now thinking of the loss of property involved, immense and serious as that is, but only of the wanton and wholesale destruction of the lives of non-combatants, men, women, and children, engaged in pursuits which have always, even in the darkest periods of modern history, been deemed innocent and legitimate. Property can be paid for; the lives of peaceful and innocent people cannot be. The present German submarine warfare against commerce is a warfare against mankind.

6. It is a war against all nations. American ships have been sunk, American lives taken, in ways which it has stirred us very deeply to learn of, but the ships and people of other neutral and friendly nations have been sunk and overwhelmed in the waters in the same way. There has been no discrimination. . . .

7. There is one choice we cannot make, we are incapable of making: we will not choose the path of submission and suffer the most sacred rights of our Nation and our people to be ignored or violated. The wrongs against which we now array ourselves are no common wrongs; they cut to the very roots of human life.

8. With a profound sense of the solemn and even tragic character of the step I am taking and of the grave responsibilities which it involves, but in unhesitating obedience to what I deem my constitutional duty, I advise that the Congress declare the recent course of the Imperial German Government to be in fact nothing less than war against the government and people of the United States; that it formally accept the status of

World War I (Page 2)

belligerent which has thus been thrust upon it; and that it take immediate steps not only to put the country in a more thorough state of defense but also to exert all its power and employ all its resources to bring the Government of the German Empire to terms and end the war. . . .

9. Our object now, as then, is to vindicate the principles of peace and justice in the life of the world as against selfish and autocratic [tyrannical] power and to set up amongst the really free and self-governed peoples of the world such a concert of purpose and of action as will henceforth insure the observance of those principles.

10. Neutrality is no longer feasible or desirable where the peace of the world is involved and the freedom of its people, and the menace to that peace and freedom lies in the existence of autocratic governments backed by organized force which is controlled wholly by their will, not by the will of their people. . . .

11. The world must be made safe for democracy. Its peace must be planted upon the tested foundations of political liberty. We have no selfish ends to serve. We desire no conquest, no dominion. We seek no indemnities for ourselves, no material compensation for the sacrifices we shall freely make. We are but one of the champions of the rights of mankind. We shall be satisfied when those rights have been made as secure as the faith and the freedom of nations can make them.
. . .

12. It is a distressing and oppressive duty, Gentlemen of the Congress, which I have performed in thus addressing you. There are, it may be, many months of fiery trial and sacrifice ahead of us. It is a fearful thing to lead this great peaceful people into war, into the most terrible and disastrous of all wars, civilization itself seeming to be in the balance.

13. But the right is more precious than peace, and we shall fight for the things which we have always carried nearest our hearts - for democracy, for the right of those who submit to authority to have a voice in their own Governments, for the rights and liberties of small nations, for a universal dominion of right by such a concert of free peoples as shall bring peace and safety to all nations and make the world itself at last free.

14. To such a task we can dedicate our lives and our fortunes, everything that we are and everything that we have, with the pride of those who know that the day has come when America is privileged to spend her blood and her might for the principles that gave her birth and happiness and the peace which she has treasured. God helping her, she can do no other.

Source: Woodrow Wilson Presidential Library

Name _____   Date _____

CHAPTER 5 ACTIVITY MASTER

World War I (Page 3)

Comprehension Questions

1. In paragraph 1, why does President Wilson say he has called this "extraordinary" session of Congress?

2. In paragraph 2, what was the extraordinary announcement that Germany had made?

3. In paragraph 3, what terrible act does President Wilson describe?

4. What international practice does President Wilson describe in paragraph 4?

5. In paragraph 5, what does President Wilson say cannot be paid for?

6. In paragraph 6, does President Wilson say only Americans have been targeted?

7. What choice does President Wilson say we cannot make in paragraph 7?

8. What does President Wilson call for in paragraph 8?

9. In paragraph 9, how does President Wilson characterize two contrasting ways of governing?

10. What does it mean in paragraph 10 when President Wilson says, "Neutrality is no longer feasible"?

World War I (Page 4)

11. In paragraph 11, what does President Wilson say we seek?

12. What does President Wilson predict will happen in the next few months?

13. In paragraph 13, what is more precious than peace?

14. How does President Wilson compare America in 1917 to America's beginnings?

Critical Thinking Questions

1. Evaluate President Wilson's persuasiveness to Congress.

2. Do you think declaring war against Germany was warranted?

3. What is President Wilson's view of the United States' responsibility to other countries?

4. Can you think of another way to solve the problem of Germany's hostile actions?

Name _____   Date _____

CHAPTER 5 ACTIVITY MASTER

League of Nations (Page 1)

Objective: 5.5.spi.7
Accompanies Student Edition p. 169

Directions: Read the following excerpt and answer the questions that follow.

Final Address in the Support of League of Nations
Delivered September 25, 1919

Do not think of this treaty of peace as merely a settlement with Germany. It is that. It is a very severe settlement with Germany, but there is not anything in it that she did not earn. Indeed, she earned more than she can ever be able to pay for, and the punishment exacted of her is not a punishment greater than she can bear, and it is absolutely necessary in order that no other nation may ever plot such a thing against humanity and civilization. But the treaty is so much more than that. It is not merely a settlement with Germany; it is a readjustment of those great injustices which underlie the whole structure of European and Asiatic society. This is only the first of several treaties. They are all constructed upon the same plan. The Austrian treaty follows the same lines. The treaty with Hungary follows the same lines. The treaty with Bulgaria follows the same lines. The treaty with Turkey, when it is formulated, will follow the same lines.

What are those lines? They are based upon the purpose to see that every government dealt with in this great settlement is put in the hands of the people and taken out of the hands of coteries and of sovereigns, who had no right to rule over the people. It is a people's treaty, that accomplishes by a great sweep of practical justice the liberation of men who never could have liberated themselves, and the power of the most powerful nations has been devoted not to their aggrandizement but to the liberation of people whom they could have put under their control if they had chosen to do so. . . .   The men who sat around the table in Paris knew that the time had come when the people were no longer going to consent to live under masters, but were going to live the lives that they chose themselves, to live under such governments as they chose themselves to erect. That is the fundamental principle of this great settlement.

1. Which countries does Wilson list?

   _____

   _____

2. Why does he say this is not just a settlement with Germany?

   _____

   _____

3. What does the word "coterie" mean in the second paragraph?

   _____

   _____

League of Nations (Page 2)

4. Make inferences as to what "those great injustices which underlie the whole structure of European and Asiatic society" means in the first paragraph.

5. Draw conclusions about what the word "aggrandizement" means.

6. What is the fundamental principle that President Wilson speaks of in the last line?

7. What is the purpose of this speech?

8. Have President Wilson's ideas been put into practice today?

9. Evaluate whether President Wilson should have put so much energy into the League of Nations.

10. If you could ask President Wilson any question about the League of Nations, what would it be?

Name _____ Date _____

CHAPTER 5 ACTIVITY MASTER

Lesson 3 Reading Guide (Page 1)
Objectives: 5.1.spi.2, 5.4.spi.2, 5.4.spi.3, 5.6.spi.1, 5.6.spi.3
Accompanies Student Edition pp. 170-177

Part I: Vocabulary
Directions: Complete the graphic organizer for the word "suffragist." Fill in the web with the definition and people and ideas associated with the word. An example has been done for you.

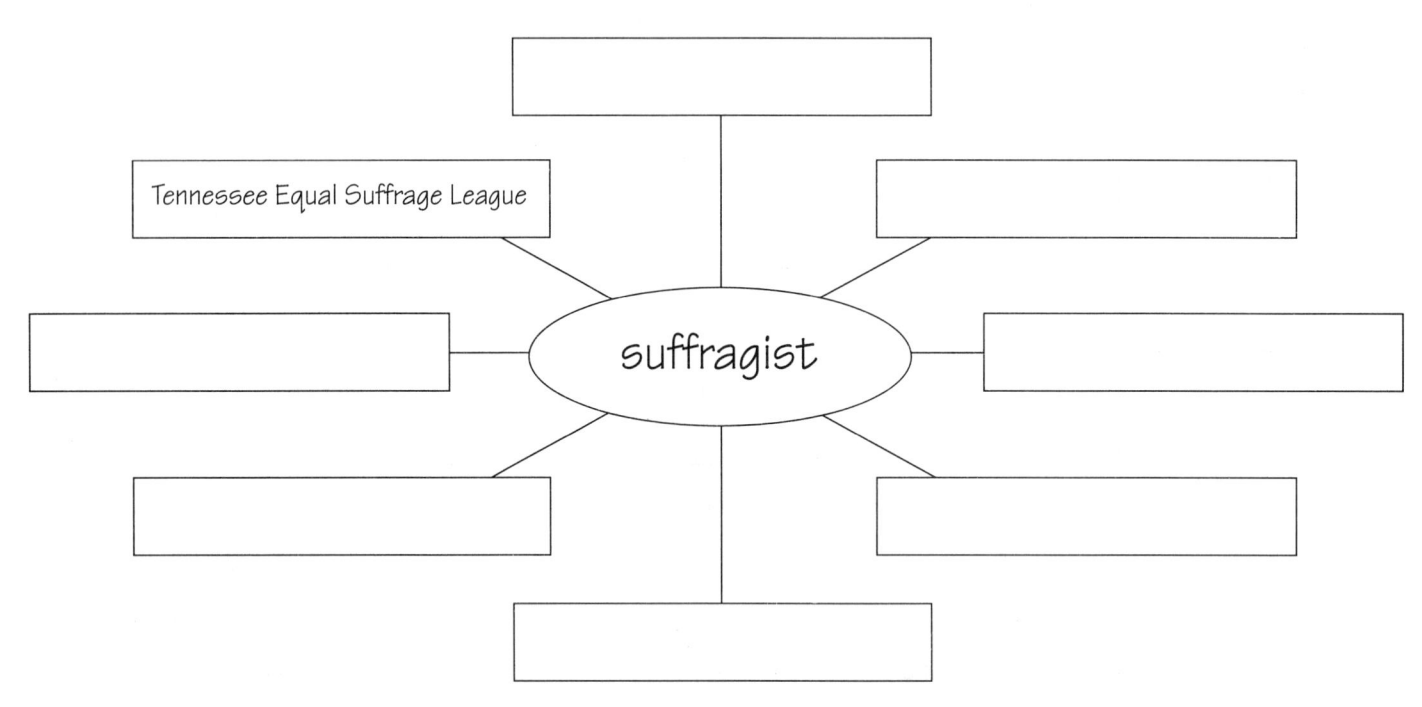

[Graphic organizer web with "suffragist" in center oval, surrounded by boxes. One box filled in: "Tennessee Equal Suffrage League"]

Part II: People to Know
Directions: Match the person to the correct quote.

____ 1. Harry T. Burn

____ 2. Albert Roberts

____ 3. Anne Dallas Dudley

____ 4. Catherine Kinney

____ 5. J. Frankie Pierce

____ 6. Abby Crawford Milton

____ 7. Josephine Pearson

A. "The battle for women's suffrage that summer, that very hot summer of 1920, in Nashville is … the fiercest legislative battle ever waged on this continent."
B. "We want to be the Perfect 36."
C. "I will hold a special session to consider the Suffrage Amendment after the primary election."
D. "Mother, I will do whatever I can to stop suffrage in Tennessee. I will wear three red roses."
E. "Dear Son, Hurrah and vote for suffrage! … Don't forget to be a good boy and help … put the 'rat' in ratification."
F. "Suffrage is only one spoke in the wheel of progress, but it is as necessary as any other … women must be free for her own sake first … and then for the sake of the whole world."
G. "My friends Anne Dallas Dudley and Abby Milton campaigned with me across the state, saying, 'Vote for Governor Albert Roberts!'"

© 2008 Gibbs Smith, Publisher
Accompanies *Tennessee Through Time: The Later Years*

Name _____   Date _____

CHAPTER 5 ACTIVITY MASTER

Lesson 3 Reading Guide (Page 2)

Part III: Short Answer

Directions: Answer the questions using your textbook.

1. What prompted women to push for equal rights in the workplace and in government?
   _____

2. What was the difference between suffragists and anti-suffragists?
   _____

3. Identify three women who fought for equal rights in Tennessee.
   _____

4. How did Harry T. Burn cause the "Perfect 36"?
   _____

Part IV: Memory Master

1. What is women's suffrage?
   _____
   _____

2. What were the arguments for and against women's suffrage?
   _____
   _____

3. How did the Nineteenth Amendment finally get passed?
   _____
   _____

Part V: Constructed Response

Directions: Answer the question using critical thinking skills.

What is the Nineteenth Amendment? What were the challenges to passing this amendment?
_____
_____

Part VI: Note Home

Lesson 3 Reading Guide is a basic overview of what the students have learned in Chapter 5 pp. 170-177. The Memory Master questions and the Constructed Response are indicators of student comprehension. For supplemental activities, see experiencestatehistory.com and click on Tennessee. Check with the teacher for the student login password.

© 2008 Gibbs Smith, Publisher
Accompanies *Tennessee Through Time: The Later Years*

Name _____   Date _____

CHAPTER 5 ACTIVITY MASTER

Problem-Solution Frame
Objective: 5.6.spi.3
Accompanies Student Edition pp. 142-179

Directions: Fill in the chart using one problem from Chapter 5.

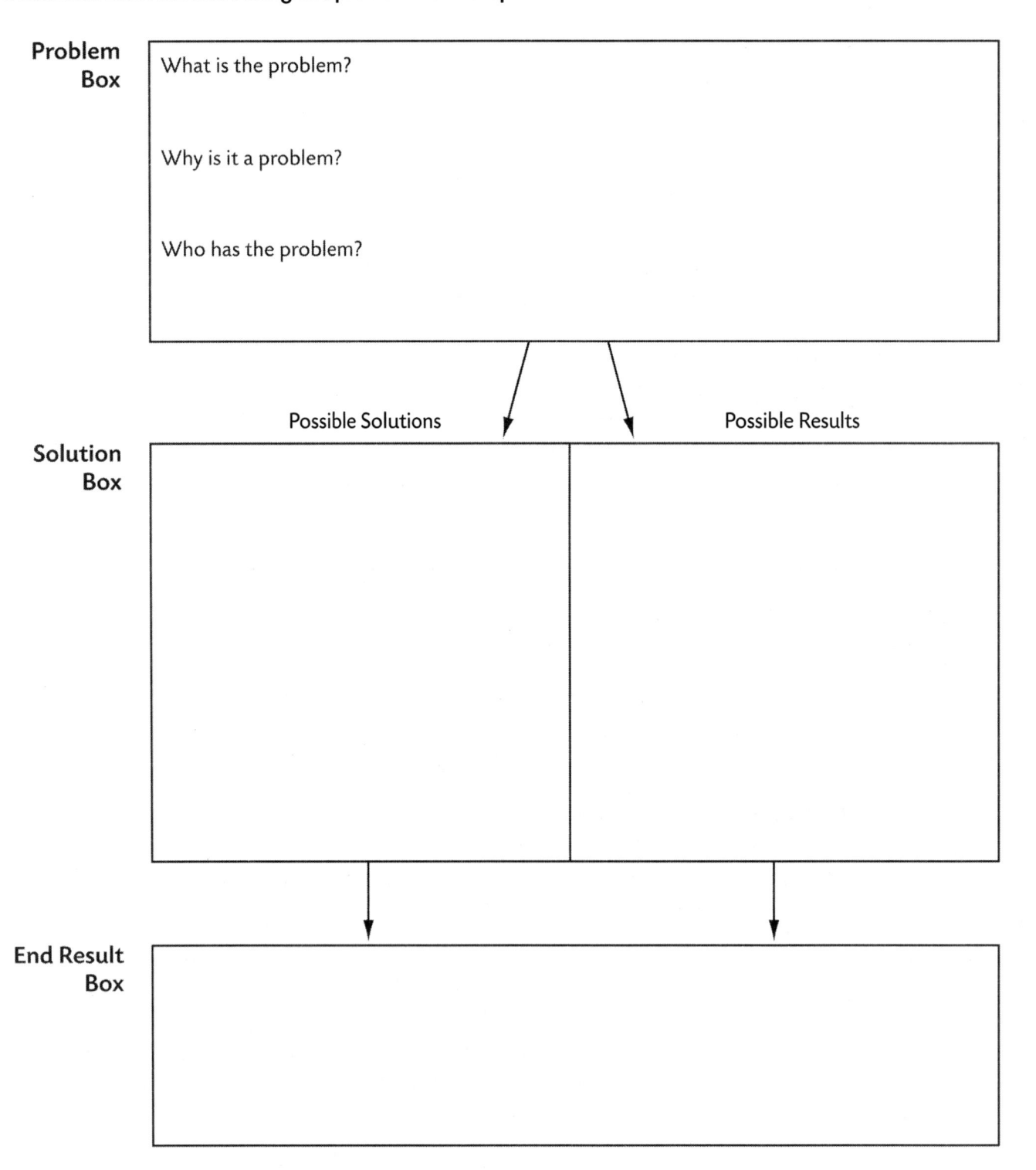

Problem Box

What is the problem?

Why is it a problem?

Who has the problem?

Solution Box

Possible Solutions | Possible Results

End Result Box

Name _____   Date _____

CHAPTER 5 REVIEW

Chapter Review Study Guide

Objectives: 5.1.spi.1, 5.1.spi.2, 5.1.spi.3, 5.4.spi.3, 5.5.spi.7, 5.6.spi.1, 5.6.spi.2
Accompanies Student Edition pp. 140-179

Part I: Vocabulary
Directions: Study the following terms. You may also use your Lesson Reading Guides.

boycott	industrialization	settlement house	draft
conservation	Jim Crow laws	stockyard	neutral
corruption	labor laws	textile	submarine
distillery	pardon	utility	truce
editorial	seamstress	alliance	suffragist

Part II: Review the following ideas for constructed and extended response.

- Define the Progressive Era.
- What progress was made for women's rights?
- Explain how automobiles affected U.S. culture.
- Identify one reason that progress was needed to improve the lives of African Americans.
- Name three things people wanted to reform during the Progressive Era.
- Explain how the terms "wet" and "dry" connect to Prohibition.
- What were Jim Crow laws?
- How did industrialization inspire progressive changes?
- What started World War I?
- Identify one reason the United States wanted to stay neutral.
- Why was World War I called a "modern war"?
- How did Americans help in the war effort?
- Identify the new underwater invention the Germans used in World War I.
- How did Tennesseans help in the war effort?
- Why did Woodrow Wilson want to form the League of Nations?
- Describe President Wilson's plan for world peace. Did it succeed?
- What prompted women to push for equal rights in the workplace and in government?
- What was the difference between suffragists and anti-suffragists?
- Identify three women who fought for equal rights in Tennessee.
- How did Harry T. Burn cause the "Perfect 36"?
- What is women's suffrage?
- What were the arguments for and against women's suffrage?
- How did the Nineteenth Amendment finally get passed?
- What is the Nineteenth Amendment? What were the challenges to passing this amendment?

© 2008 Gibbs Smith, Publisher
Accompanies *Tennessee Through Time: The Later Years*

CHAPTER 6 TABLE OF CONTENTS

Chapter 6
Good Times and Hard Times in Tennessee (Student Edition pp. 180-217)

Table of Contents			
Activity Master	Standard Correlation	Page #	Accompanies Student Edition pages
Lesson 1 Reading Guide	5.1.spi.1, 5.1.spi.2	96-98	182-191
Lesson 2 Reading Guide	5.2.spi.2, 5.4.spi.2, 5.6.spi.1	99-101	192-197
Lesson 3 Reading Guide	5.2.spi.3, 5.2.spi.4, 5.2.spi.5, 5.2.spi.6	102-105	198-207
Passport to History	5.2.spi.6	106-107	199
Lesson 4 Reading Guide	5.2.spi.3, 5.2.spi.4, 5.2.spi.5, 5.6.spi.3	108-110	208-215
ELL: Fill in the Blank	5.1.spi.2, 5.5.spi.3	111	182-215
Chapter Review	5.1.spi.1, 5.1.spi.2, 5.2.spi.3, 5.2.spi.4, 5.2.spi.5, 5.4.spi.2, 5.6.spi.1	112-113	180-217

© 2008 Gibbs Smith, Publisher
Accompanies *Tennessee Through Time: The Later Years*

Name _____   Date _____

CHAPTER 6 ACTIVITY MASTER

Lesson 1 Reading Guide (Page 1)
Objectives: 5.1.spi.1, 5.1.spi.2
Accompanies Student Edition pp. 182-191

Part I: Vocabulary

Directions: Write in a category title to fit each group of words.

Category #1: _____
   gramophone
   phonograph

Category #2: _____
   nickelodeon

Category #3: _____
   blues
   ragtime

Category #4: _____
   navigation

Part II: People to Know

Directions: Write one fact about each person. Then write one important thing you think that person might have said.

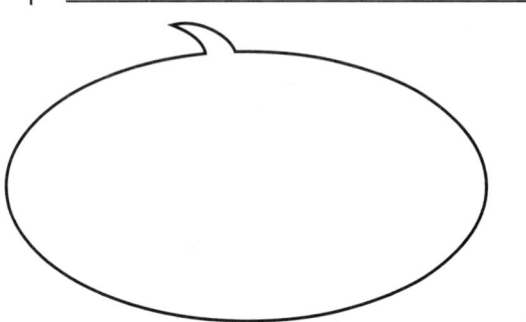

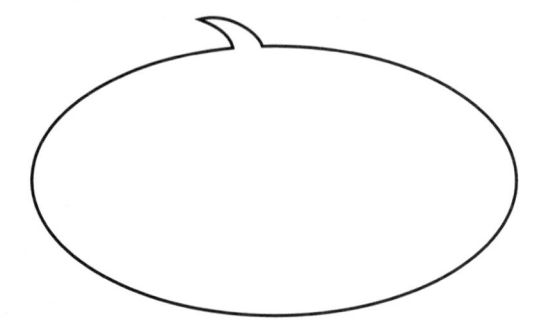

1. Ed Crump: _____

2. Thomas Edison: _____

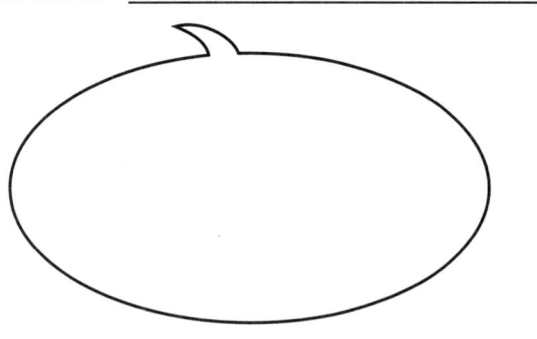

3. W. C. Handy: _____

4. Charles A. Lindbergh: _____

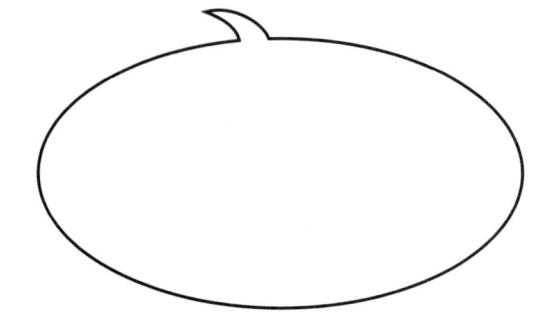

96

© 2008 Gibbs Smith, Publisher
Accompanies *Tennessee Through Time: The Later Years*

Name _____   Date _____

CHAPTER 6 ACTIVITY MASTER

Lesson 1 Reading Guide (Page 2)

5. Robert Neyland: _____

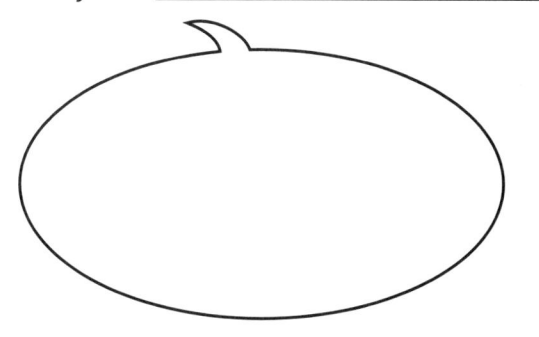

7. Bessie Smith: _____

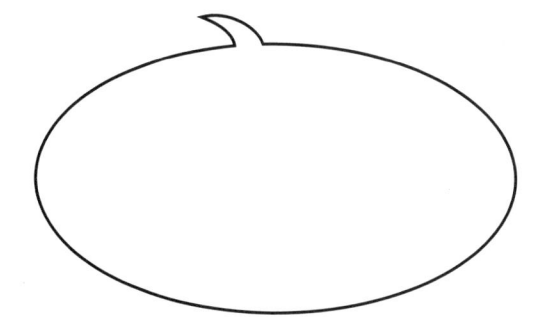

6. Clarence Saunders: _____

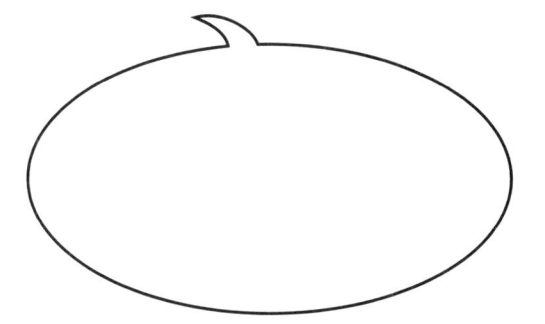

8. James D. Vaughan: _____

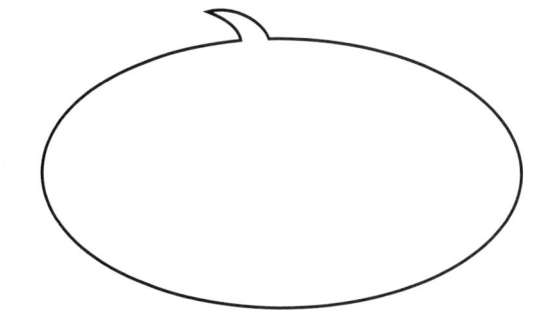

Part III: Short Answer

Directions: Answer the questions using your textbook.

1. How were ragtime and the blues part of the culture?
   _____
   _____

2. During the Roaring Twenties, what was the relationship between technology and entertainment?
   _____
   _____

3. How is the *Grand Ole Opry* part of Tennessee history?
   _____
   _____

4. How did Charles Lindbergh and Clarence Saunders change society?
   _____
   _____

Name _____ Date _____

CHAPTER 6 ACTIVITY MASTER

Lesson 1 Reading Guide (Page 3)

Part IV: Memory Master

1. Describe the period known as the Roaring Twenties.
   _____
   _____

2. Name one form of entertainment that first appeared during this period of history.
   _____
   _____

3. Who was Charles Lindbergh? What great feat did he accomplish?
   _____
   _____

Part V: Constructed Response

Directions: Answer the question using critical thinking skills.

Describe life during the Roaring Twenties using three examples.
_____
_____

Part VI: Note Home

Lesson 1 Reading Guide is a basic overview of what the students have learned in Chapter 6 pp. 182-191. The Memory Master questions and the Constructed Response are indicators of student comprehension. For supplemental activities, see experiencestatehistory.com and click on Tennessee. Check with the teacher for the student login password.

Name _____   Date _____

CHAPTER 6 ACTIVITY MASTER

Lesson 2 Reading Guide (Page 1)
Objectives: 5.2.spi.2, 5.4.spi.2, 5.6.spi.1
Accompanies Student Edition pp. 192-197

Part I: Vocabulary
Directions: Define each word and explain how the words are connected.

1. evolution: _____

2. evolve: _____

Connection: _____
_____
_____

Part II: People to Know
Directions: Match the person to the correct description.

_____ 1. Clarence Darrow

_____ 2. William Jennings Bryan

_____ 3. John T. Scopes

_____ 4. John Washington Butler

_____ 5. Austin Peay

_____ 6. Woodrow Wilson

A. He was a high school teacher who taught human evolution so he could get arrested.

B. He was a famous criminal lawyer for Scopes.

C. He became governor when Tennessee was in debt and turned the state's money into a surplus.

D. He was the lawyer who represented the state in the Scopes trial.

E. He introduced a bill to prohibit the teaching of human evolution in all public schools in Tennessee.

F. His secretary of state had run for president three times.

Name _____ Date _____

CHAPTER 6 ACTIVITY MASTER

Lesson 2 Reading Guide (Page 2)

Part III: Places to Locate

Directions: On the map, locate and label the following location. Then answer the question.

Dayton

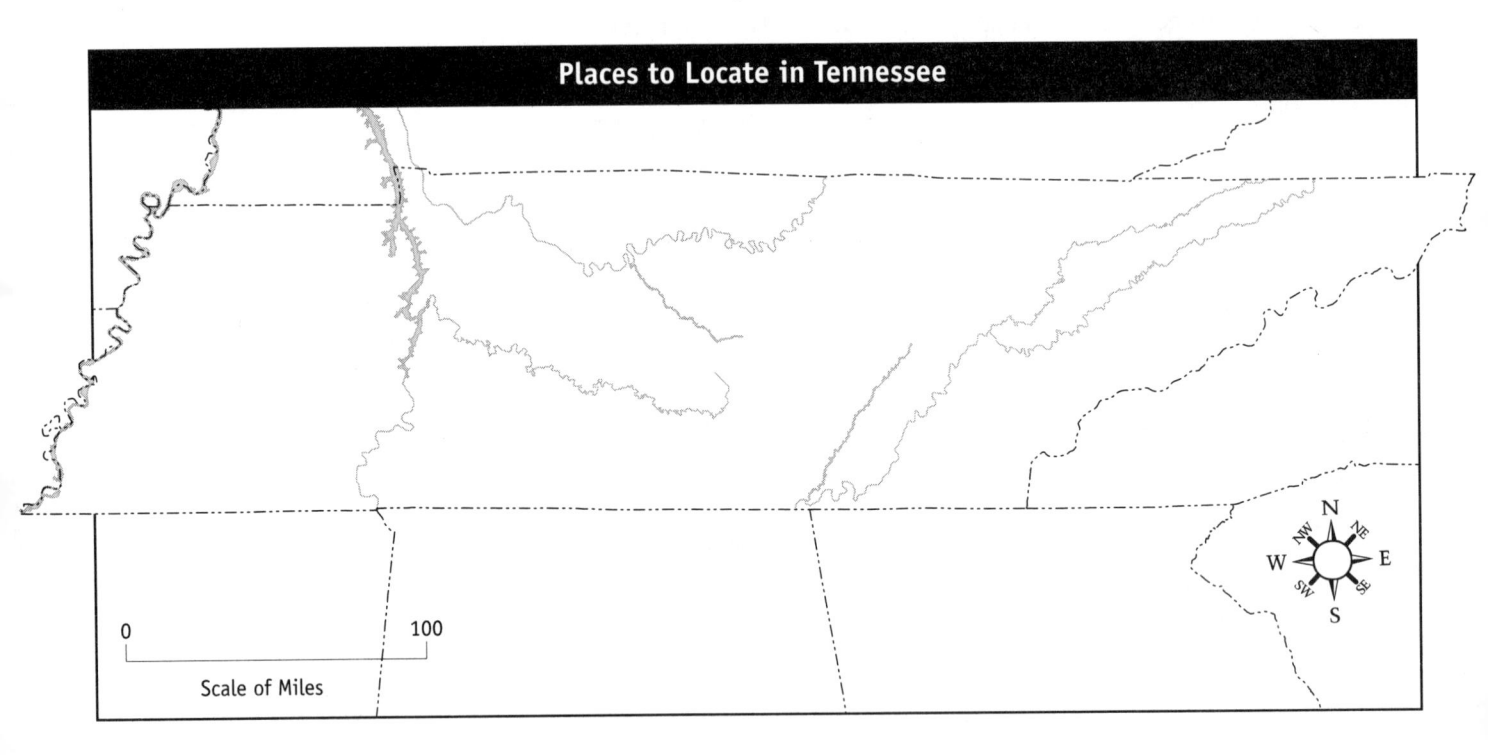

Places to Locate in Tennessee

What is significant about Dayton in this chapter?

_____
_____
_____
_____

© 2008 Gibbs Smith, Publisher
Accompanies *Tennessee Through Time: The Later Years*

Name _____   Date _____

CHAPTER 6 ACTIVITY MASTER

Lesson 2 Reading Guide (Page 3)

Part IV: Short Answer

Directions: Answer the questions using complete sentences.

1. How did Governor Austin Peay turn the state's debt into a surplus?
   _____
   _____

2. Give one example each for how Governor Peay improved schools and roads.
   _____

3. What were some of the different views in Tennessee about human evolution?
   _____
   _____

4. Why did some men at Robinson's Drug Store think that a local trial about human evolution would be good for their town? _____
   _____

Part V: Memory Master

1. Identify Governor Austin Peay's two main areas of concern. _____
   _____

2. What was the Butler Act? _____
   _____

3. Summarize how the Scopes trial ended. _____
   _____

Part VI: Constructed Response

Directions: Answer the question using critical thinking skills.

Do you think the Scopes trial had a positive effect on Tennessee? Why or why not?
_____
_____

Part VII: Note Home

Lesson 2 Reading Guide is a basic overview of what the students have learned in Chapter 6 pp. 192-197. The Memory Master questions and the Constructed Response are indicators of student comprehension. For supplemental activities, see experiencestatehistory.com and click on Tennessee. Check with the teacher for the student login password.

© 2008 Gibbs Smith, Publisher
Accompanies *Tennessee Through Time: The Later Years*

Name _____ Date _____

CHAPTER 6 ACTIVITY MASTER

Lesson 3 Reading Guide (Page 1)

Objectives: 5.2.spi.3, 5.2.spi.4, 5.2.spi.5, 5.2.spi.6
Accompanies Student Edition pp. 198-207

Part I: Vocabulary

Directions: Write a poem that uses each vocabulary word at least once. You may add prefixes or suffixes to the vocabulary words.

    credit   debt   Great Depression   interest   stock market   tear gas   topsoil

Lesson 3 Reading Guide (Page 2)

Part II: People to Know

Directions: Circle the correct response.

1. What was Herbert Hoover's view of government?
   - A He thought the government should let businesses operate without a lot of laws.
   - B He helped pass many laws that would restrict business and end poverty.
   - C He told Americans that the U.S. government was in perfect condition.
   - D He thought that bad things were about to happen to the U.S. economy, so the government needed more agencies to help.

2. What was Henry Horton's role in the Elizabethton Strikes of 1929?
   - A mill owner
   - B striker
   - C governor
   - D worker

3. What was Margaret Bowen's role in the Elizabethton Strikes of 1929?
   - A She organized a union.
   - B She led the striking female workers.
   - C She was the mill owner.
   - D She was the lawyer called in to solve the problem.

4. How did Edward Crump keep the Union Planters Bank open?
   - A He ordered bank workers to pile up money on the counters so people could see there was still plenty.
   - B He had the bank close for three weeks so no one could take out any money.
   - C He told the bank workers to strike.
   - D He went to the bank and deposited half a million dollars.

5. How did DeFord Bailey help people during the Great Depression?
   - A He donated money to the Hoovervilles.
   - B He went to Nashville to find work.
   - C His music on the *Grand Ole Opry* brought people some happiness.
   - D He dedicated his music to finding a cure for poverty.

Name _____   Date _____

CHAPTER 6 ACTIVITY MASTER

Lesson 3 Reading Guide (Page 3)

Part III: Places to Locate

Directions: Describe the geographical location and historical significance of the following locations.

1. Elizabethton

    Geographical location _____

    Historical significance _____

2. Great Plains

    Geographical location _____

    Historical significance _____

Part IV: Short Answer

Directions: Answer the questions using complete sentences.

1. What conditions in the U.S. economy led to the Great Depression?

    _____

    _____

2. What were some of the effects of the Dust Bowl?

    _____

    _____

3. Describe how a run on the bank occurred.

    _____

    _____

4. How did buying on credit cause people in the 1920s to have interest?

    _____

    _____

Name _____ Date _____

CHAPTER 6 ACTIVITY MASTER

Lesson 3 Reading Guide (Page 4)

Part V: Memory Master

1. Explain how buying on credit works.
   _____
   _____

2. What did the Elizabethton strikes become a model for?
   _____
   _____

3. How did the stock market crash cause the Great Depression?
   _____
   _____

Part VI: Constructed Response

Directions: Answer the question using critical thinking skills.

What do you think Americans experienced during the Great Depression and the Dust Bowl?
   _____
   _____

Part VII: Note Home

Lesson 3 Reading Guide is a basic overview of what the students have learned in Chapter 6 pp. 198-207. The Memory Master questions and the Constructed Response are indicators of student comprehension. For supplemental activities, see experiencestatehistory.com and click on Tennessee. Check with the teacher for the student login password.

Name _____ Date _____

CHAPTER 6 ACTIVITY MASTER

Passport to History (Page 1)

Objective: 5.2.spi.6
Accompanies Student Edition p. 199

Teacher Initial _____

Date _____

Part I: Interest Today

Directions: Make a list of ways we use interest today.

_____
_____
_____
_____
_____
_____

Part II: Examples of Interest Percentages

Directions: Ask an adult for an example of what percentage interest is on a home loan or credit card purchase.

_____
_____
_____

Part III: Advertisements

Directions: List advertisements that try to get people to purchase on credit.

_____
_____
_____
_____
_____
_____

Name _____ Date _____

CHAPTER 6 ACTIVITY MASTER

Passport to History (Page 2)

Part IV: Retail Credit Math

Directions: Solve the math problem.

Pretend a family wanted to buy a home that cost $100,000. But the family only had $10,000. They paid $10,000 to the home owner and borrowed the rest from the bank.

1. How much did the family have to borrow from the bank? _____

2. If the family had to pay $1,000 a month to the bank, how many months would it take to pay back the loan?
   _____

3. Now think about interest on the loan. If the bank charged 10 percent interest on the loan, how much would the interest be? _____

4. How many more months would it take to pay off the interest? _____

5. This is a very simple example of interest. Today, banks charge interest on each month of a loan, not just the original loan amount. Circle the correct choice about interest:

   When you borrow money with interest to make a purchase, you end up paying _____ the original price.

   A much less than
   B the same as
   C a tiny bit more than
   D much more than

© 2008 Gibbs Smith, Publisher
Accompanies *Tennessee Through Time: The Later Years*

Name _____ Date _____

CHAPTER 6 ACTIVITY MASTER

Lesson 4 Reading Guide (Page 1)

Objectives: 5.2.spi.3, 5.2.spi.4, 5.2.spi.5, 5.6.spi.3
Accompanies Student Edition pp. 208-215

Part I: Vocabulary

Directions: Fill in the chart.

Word	Page Number	Definition	What it means in Lesson 4
auditor			
tributary			

Part II: People to Know

Directions: Write one main idea about each person. Then answer the questions that follow.

1. Joseph Wellington Byrns: _____

2. Frieda Carter: _____

3. Garnet Carter: _____

4. Herbert Hoover: _____

5. George Norris: _____

6. Franklin Delano Roosevelt: _____

A. Which two of these people disagreed about the Great Depression?
_____

B. Which three of these people agreed upon New Deal programs?
_____

C. Which two of these people worked together to earn money during the depression?
_____

© 2008 Gibbs Smith, Publisher
Accompanies *Tennessee Through Time: The Later Years*

Name _____   Date _____

CHAPTER 6 ACTIVITY MASTER

Lesson 4 Reading Guide (Page 2)

Part III: Places to Locate

Directions: Locate each place on the map of Tennessee. Then answer the question.

    Crossville   Rock City   Smoky Mountains   Tennessee River Valley

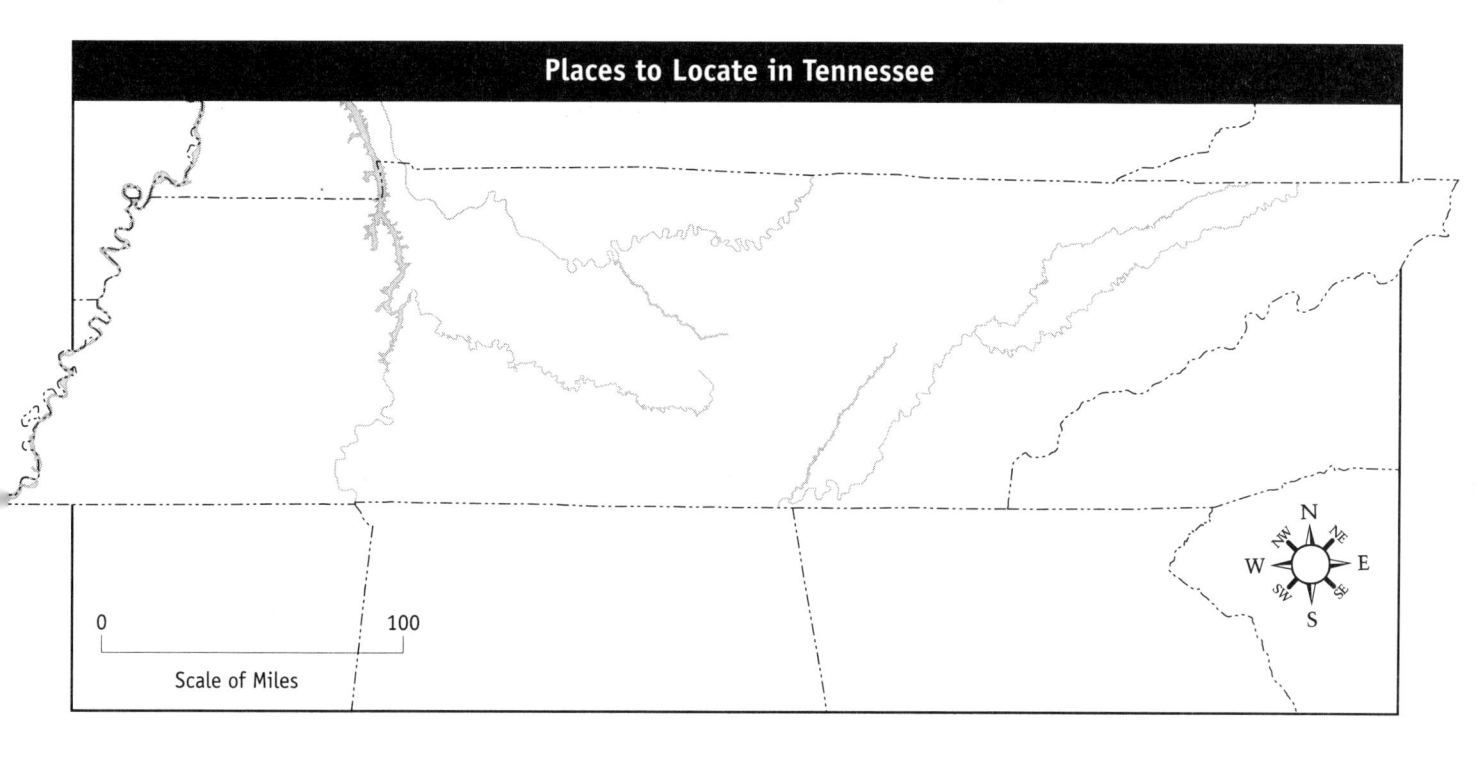

Places to Locate in Tennessee

What do these locations all have in common? Explain.

_____
_____
_____
_____
_____
_____

© 2008 Gibbs Smith, Publisher
Accompanies *Tennessee Through Time: The Later Years*

Lesson 4 Reading Guide (Page 3)

Part IV: Short Answer

Directions: Answer the questions using complete sentences.

1. Why did Roosevelt win the presidential election by a landslide?

2. What were the first "Hundred Days"?

3. How did the TVA help Tennessee?

4. Was the Great Depression over once the New Deal began? Why or why not?

Part V: Memory Master

1. Who won the 1932 presidential election?

2. Describe the New Deal.

3. Name two New Deal programs that helped Tennessee pull out of the Great Depression.

Part VI: Constructed Response

Directions: Answer the question using critical thinking skills.

Describe what life was like in Tennessee before and after the TVA (Tennessee Valley Authority).

Part VII: Note Home

Lesson 4 Reading Guide is a basic overview of what the students have learned in Chapter 6 pp. 208-215. The Memory Master questions and the Constructed Response are indicators of student comprehension. For supplemental activities, see experiencestatehistory.com and click on Tennessee. Check with the teacher for the student login

Name _____   Date _____

CHAPTER 6 ACTIVITY MASTER

ELL: Fill in the Blank

Objectives: 5.1.spi.2, 5.5.spi.3
Accompanies Student Edition pp. 182-215

Directions: Fill in the blanks with the correct response. Use the page numbers to help you find information.

Lesson 1 The 1920s

1. The Roaring Twenties was a time when there seemed to be plenty of _____. (p. 182)
2. People could enjoy entertainment like _____, _____, and _____ _____. (pp. 182-185)
3. Tennessee radio started a program called The _____ _____ _____. (p. 186)
4. Charles Lindbergh flew across the _____ Ocean. (p. 188)

Lesson 2 A Time of Change

5. Governor Austin Peay improved Tennessee's _____ and _____ (pp. 192-193).
6. The Scopes trial was about teaching _____ in schools. (p. 194)

Lesson 3 The Stock Market Crash

7. People could buy things on _____ and owe _____ on the loan. (p. 198)
8. When many stocks were sold at once, the _____ _____ crashed. (p. 200)
9. Mill workers went on _____ in Elizabethton in 1929. (p. 201)
10. The time when people did not have jobs, money, or food is called the _____ _____ (p. 202)
11. The Dust Bowl happened on the Great Plains when there was little rain, heat, wind, and nothing to hold the _____ in place. (p. 204)

Lesson 4 FDR's New Deal

12. When Roosevelt was 39 years old, he got a disease called _____ that left him in a _____ the rest of his life. (p. 208)
13. Roosevelt promised the American people a _____ _____. (p. 209)
14. Some New Deal programs that helped Tennessee were the following. Write out the abbreviations:

    AAA _____ (p. 211)

    TVA _____ (p. 212)

    CCC _____ (p. 214)

© 2008 Gibbs Smith, Publisher
Accompanies *Tennessee Through Time: The Later Years*

Name _____ Date _____

CHAPTER 6 REVIEW

Chapter Review Study Guide

Objectives: 5.1.spi.1, 5.1.spi.2, 5.2.spi.3, 5.2.spi.4, 5.2.spi.5, 5.4.spi.2, 5.6.spi.1
Accompanies Student Edition pp. 180-217

Part I: Vocabulary

Directions: Study the following terms. You may also use your Lesson Reading Guides.

blues	ragtime	Great Depression	auditor
gramophone	evolution	interest	tributary
navigation	evolve	stock market	
nickelodeon	credit	tear gas	
phonograph	debt	topsoil	

Part II: Review the following ideas for constructed and extended response.

- How were ragtime and the blues part of the culture?
- During the Roaring Twenties, what was the relationship between technology and entertainment?
- How is the Grand Ole Opry part of Tennessee history?
- How did someone like Charles Lindbergh or Clarence Saunders change society?
- Describe the period known as the Roaring Twenties.
- Name one form of entertainment that first appeared during this period of history.
- Who was Charles Lindbergh? What great feat did he accomplish?
- Describe life during the Roaring Twenties using three examples.
- Identify Governor Austin Peay's two main areas of concern.
- What was the Butler Act?
- Summarize how the Scopes trial ended.
- How did Governor Austin Peay turn the state's debt into a surplus?
- Give one example each for how Governor Peay improved schools and roads.
- What were some of the different views in Tennessee about human evolution?
- Why did some men at Robinson's Drug Store think that a local trial about human evolution would be good for their town?
- Do you think the Scopes trial had a positive effect on Tennessee?
- What conditions in the U.S. economy led to the Great Depression?
- What were some of the effects of the Dust Bowl?
- Describe how a run on the bank occurred.
- How did buying on credit cause people in the 1920s to have interest?
- Explain how buying on credit works.
- What did the Elizabethton strikes become a model for?
- How did the stock market crash cause the Great Depression?
- What do you think Americans experienced during the Great Depression and the Dust Bowl?
- Why did Roosevelt win the presidential election by a landslide?
- What were the first "Hundred Days"?
- How did the TVA help Tennessee?
- Was the Great Depression over once the New Deal began? Why or why not?

Name _____   Date _____

CHAPTER 6 REVIEW

- Who won the 1932 presidential election?
- Describe the New Deal.
- Name two New Deal programs that helped Tennessee pull out of the Great Depression.
- Describe what life was like in Tennessee before and after the TVA (Tennessee Valley Authority).

Part III: Review

Cut out the following sentences on the dotted lines. Mix up the order of the sentences. Trade piles with a partner, and put the events in order from earliest to latest.

Austin Peay becomes governor of Tennessee.

The Scopes trial takes place in Dayton, Tennessee.

Charles Lindbergh flies across the Atlantic Ocean.

The stock market in New York City crashes.

The Great Depression begins.

Garnet and Frieda Carter open Rock City.

Franklin Delano Roosevelt starts the New Deal.

The Great Smoky Mountain National Park opens.

© 2008 Gibbs Smith, Publisher
Accompanies *Tennessee Through Time: The Later Years*

CHAPTER 7 TABLE OF CONTENTS

Chapter 7
World War II (Student Edition pp. 218-253)

Table of Contents			
Activity Master	**Standard Correlation**	**Page #**	**Accompanies Student Edition pages**
Lesson 1 Reading Guide	5.4.spi.2, 5.6.spi.2, 5.6.spi.3	116-120	220-229
Passport to History	5.6.spi.3	121	227
Lesson 2 Reading Guide	5.1.spi.1, 5.1.spi.2	122-124	230-242
World War II	5.6.spi.2	125	230-242
Fireside Chats	5.5.spi.7	126-127	237
Lesson 3 Reading Guide	5.1.spi.2, 5.5.spi.7	128-130	243-251
ELL: Taking Notes	5.1.spi.1, 5.1.spi.2, 5.4.spi.2	131	220-251
Chapter Review	5.1.spi.1, 5.1.spi.2, 5.4.spi.2, 5.5.spi.7	132	218-251

Name _____ Date _____

CHAPTER 7 ACTIVITY MASTER

Lesson 1 Reading Guide (Page 1)
Objectives: 5.4.spi.2, 5.6.spi.2, 5.6.spi.3
Accompanies Student Edition pp. 220-229

Part I: Vocabulary
Directions: Write one sentence that uses each word in the group. The first one is done for you.

1. Nazi, racial supremacy, swastika

    In Germany, the Nazi political party believed in racial supremacy, and its symbol was the swastika.

2. Axis Powers, Allied Powers

    _____
    _____

3. communism, dictator

    _____
    _____

4. concentration camp, Holocaust

    _____
    _____

5. arsenal, lease

    _____
    _____

6. hosiery, inferior

    _____
    _____

Lesson 1 Reading Guide (Page 2)

Part II: People to Know

Directions: Write what each person did during World War II.

1. Winston Churchill _____

2. Emperor Hirohito _____

3. Adolf Hitler _____

4. Jacob May _____

5. Norman Rockwell _____

6. Franklin D. Roosevelt _____

7. Wendell Wilkie _____

Name _____ Date _____

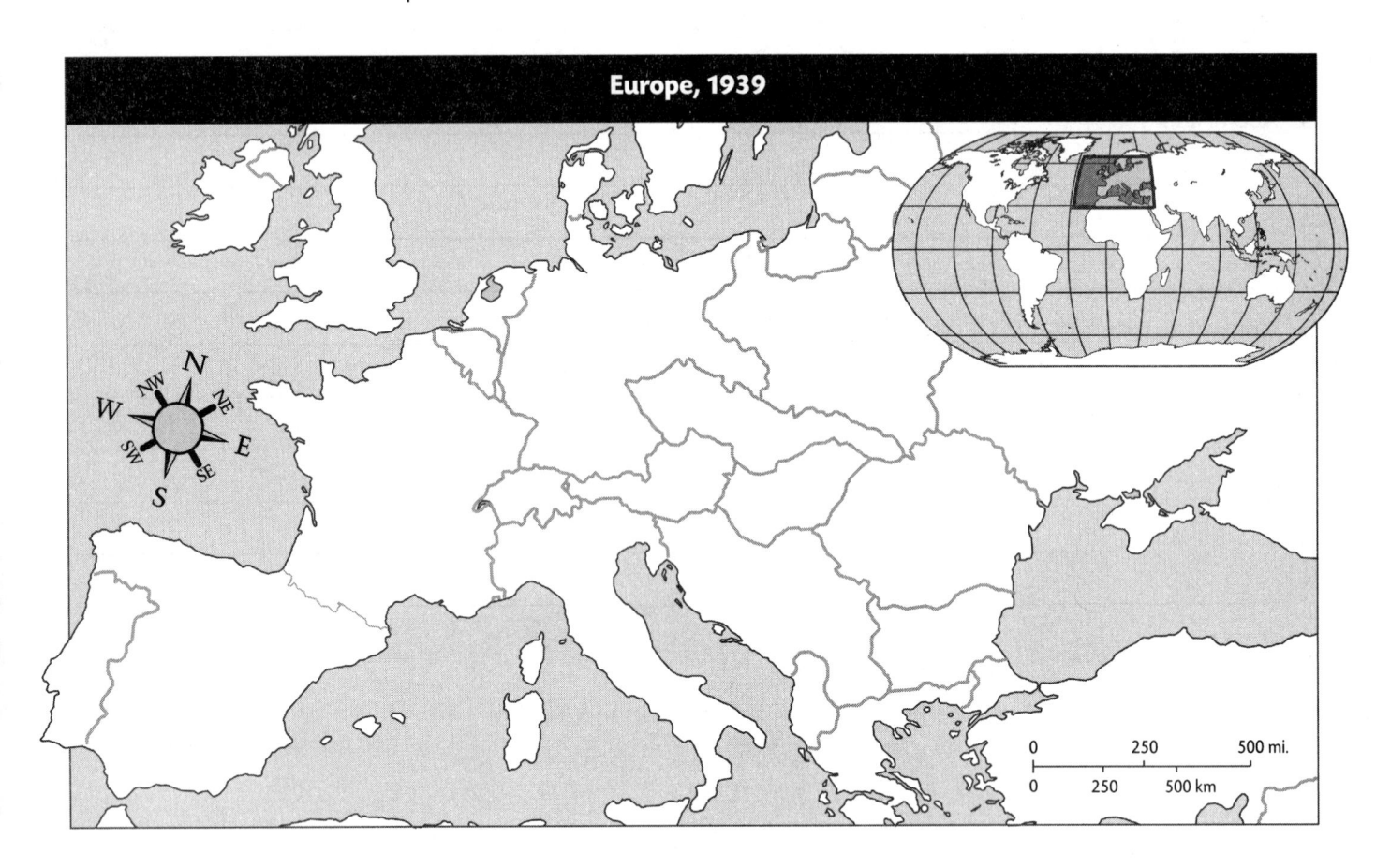

CHAPTER 7 ACTIVITY MASTER

Lesson 1 Reading Guide (Page 3)

Part III: Places to Locate

Directions: Locate and label the following countries that were part of Europe in 1939.

Belgium	Germany	The Netherlands
Czechoslovakia	Great Britain	Norway
Denmark	Italy	Poland
France	Japan	Soviet Union

Europe, 1939

Name _____   Date _____

CHAPTER 7 ACTIVITY MASTER

Lesson 1 Reading Guide (Page 4)

Part IV: Short Answer

Directions: Answer the questions using complete sentences.

1. Identify one reason Hitler rose to power.
   _____
   _____

2. What actions did the German army take in Europe?
   _____
   _____

3. Explain how the Nazi Party carried out the Holocaust.
   _____
   _____

4. Why did Roosevelt talk about the Four Freedoms when he was re-elected in 1940?
   _____
   _____

Part V: Memory Master

1. Who created concentration camps and why?
   _____
   _____

2. Which three countries formed the Axis Powers? Which three countries formed the Allied Powers?
   _____
   _____

3. Who was elected president of the United States for a third term?
   _____
   _____

Name _____   Date _____

CHAPTER 7 ACTIVITY MASTER

Lesson 1 Reading Guide (Page 5)

Part VI: Constructed Response

Directions: Answer the question using critical thinking skills.

What were some of the different points of view Americans had about entering war?

_____

_____

_____

Part VII: Note Home

Lesson 1 Reading Guide is a basic overview of what the students have learned in Chapter 7 pp. 220-229. The Memory Master questions and the Constructed Response are indicators of student comprehension. For supplemental activities, see experiencestatehistory.com and click on Tennessee. Check with the teacher for the student login password.

Name _____ Date _____

CHAPTER 7 ACTIVITY MASTER

Passport to History

Objective: 5.6.spi.3
Accompanies Student Edition p. 227

Teacher Initial _____
Date _____

Directions: Match these world leaders to their own countries by writing the country next to the name of the leader. Then answer the questions that follow.

1. Adolf Hitler _____

2. Winston Churchill _____

3. Franklin Roosevelt _____

4. Emperor Hirohito _____

Identify the differing political views of these world leaders to understand the conflict of World War II.

Adolf Hitler	Winston Churchill
Franklin Roosevelt	Emperor Hirohito

Challenge question: Name the leader of Italy who allied with Germany.

Name _____ Date _____

CHAPTER 7 ACTIVITY MASTER

Lesson 2 Reading Guide (Page 1)

Objectives: 5.1.spi.1, 5.1.spi.2
Accompanies Student Edition pp. 230-242

Part I: Vocabulary

Directions: Fill in the chart for each vocabulary word.

Word	Definition	Sample Sentence	Illustration
liberate			
rationing			

Name _____   Date _____

CHAPTER 7 ACTIVITY MASTER

Lesson 2 Reading Guide (Page 2)

Part II: People to Know

Directions: Write how each person helped the United States during World War II.

1. Roy Acuff _____

2. Prentice Cooper _____

3. Dwight D. Eisenhower _____

4. Cornelia Fort _____

5. Minnie Pearl _____

6. Franklin D. Roosevelt _____

7. Dinah Shore _____

Part III: Places to Locate

Directions: Describe how each location listed below was affected by World War II. Then locate Normandy Peninsula, France, on the world map in your book on p. 345.

1. Clarksville (p. 232) _____

2. Henry County (p. 232) _____

3. Lebanon, Tennessee (p. 233) _____

4. Pearl Harbor, Hawaii (p. 230) _____

5. Smyrna (p. 232) _____

6. Tullahoma (p. 232) _____

© 2008 Gibbs Smith, Publisher
Accompanies *Tennessee Through Time: The Later Years*

Name _____   Date _____

CHAPTER 7 ACTIVITY MASTER

Lesson 2 Reading Guide (Page 3)

Part IV: Short Answer

Directions: Answer the questions using complete sentences.

1. What made the United States determined to declare war?

2. How did Tennessee prepare for war?

3. What did Americans do to help in the war effort?

4. How did women's lives change because of World War II?

Part V: Memory Master

1. What happened on December 7, 1941?

2. Why did Americans ration during World War II? Name two items that were rationed.

3. Summarize what happened on D-Day.

Part VI: Constructed Response

Directions: Answer the question using critical thinking skills.

Draw conclusions on how World War II affected U.S. and Tennessee economy.

Part VII: Note Home

Lesson 2 Reading Guide is a basic overview of what the students have learned in Chapter 7 pp. 230-242. The Memory Master questions and the Constructed Response are indicators of student comprehension. For supplemental activities, see experiencestatehistory.com and click on Tennessee. Check with the teacher for the student login password.

Name _____   Date _____

CHAPTER 7 ACTIVITY MASTER

World War II
Objective: 5.6.spi.2
Accompanies Student Edition pp. 230-242

Directions: Read the following story and answer the questions that follow.

It was a summer day in 1942 when the German police appeared at the door of the Paluch family in Poland. They had orders to take the three-year-old twins, Adam and Ida. Their father, Chaim, was off fighting for the Polish Army. Their mother, Esther, ran off down the street, and in the confusion that followed, Aunt Rose was able to sneak the twins away. Eventually they were given new names and sent to live with two different Catholic families. That way they would be safe throughout the war.

That was the last time the twins saw each other for 53 years. Because they were separated at such an early age, they didn't even remember they had a twin. Ida ended up in Skokie, a suburb of Chicago. She had reclaimed her real name. Adam had stayed in Poland. His name was now Jerzy Dolebski.

Both twins spent their adult lives searching phone books in every city they visited for possible family members lost in the Holocaust. Then Ida's childhood friend sent her a newspaper article about a Polish Holocaust survivor who was searching for his family. Although Ida didn't recognize the name of the man in the picture, she did recognize his face because Adam looked so much like their grandfather.

Adam moved to Skokie, Illinois, to live with his twin sister. "I am like a child again," he told an interviewer. "I am a very lucky man."

1. Why were the twins separated? _____
2. Where were the twins kept to stay safe? _____
3. For how many years were the twins separated? _____
4. What did Ida and Adam do to try to find their Polish relatives? _____
   _____
5. How did Ida know Adam was her relative? _____
   _____
6. The story doesn't say what happened to other members of Ida and Adam's family. What do you think happened to them? _____
7. What other things are not in this story? _____
   _____
8. What is the theme or main meaning of this story? _____
9. What title would you give this story? _____
10. What makes this story unique? Do you think there might be other stories like this one? How would you find out?
    _____
    _____

© 2008 Gibbs Smith, Publisher
Accompanies *Tennessee Through Time: The Later Years*

Name _____ Date _____

CHAPTER 7 ACTIVITY MASTER

Fireside Chats

Objective: 5.5.spi.7
Accompanies Student Edition p. 237

Directions: The following passage is from Franklin D. Roosevelt's Fireside Chat 25 delivered on July 28, 1943. Read the excerpt from the end of his Fireside Chat and answer the questions that follow.

On Progress of War and Plans for Peace

1. The American soldier does not like the necessity of waging war. And yet—if he lays off for a single instant he may lose his own life and sacrifice the lives of his comrades.

2. By the same token—a worker here at home may not like the driving, wartime conditions under which he has to work and live. And yet—if he gets complacent or indifferent and slacks on his job, he too may sacrifice the lives of American soldiers and contribute to the loss of an important battle.

3. The next time anyone says to you that this war is "in the bag," or says "it's all over but the shouting," you should ask him these questions: "Are you working full time on your job?" "Are you growing all the food you can?" "Are you buying your limit of war bonds?" "Are you loyally and cheerfully cooperating with your Government in preventing inflation and profiteering, and in making rationing work with fairness to all?"

4. "Because—if your answer is 'No'—then the war is going to last a lot longer than you think. The plans we made for knocking out Mussolini and his gang have largely succeeded. But we still have to knock out Hitler and his gang, and Tojo and his gang. No one of us pretends that this will be an easy matter."

5. We still have to defeat Hitler and Tojo on their own home grounds. But this will require a far greater concentration of our national energy and our ingenuity and our skill.

6. It is not too much to say that we must pour into this war the entire strength and intelligence and will power of the United States. We are a great nation—a rich nation—but we are not so great or so rich that we can afford to waste our substance or the lives of our men by relaxing along the way.

7. We shall not settle for less than total victory. That is the determination of every American on the fighting fronts. That must be, and will be, the determination of every American here at home.

© 2008 Gibbs Smith, Publisher
Accompanies *Tennessee Through Time: The Later Years*

Name _____ Date _____

CHAPTER 7 ACTIVITY MASTER

Fireside Chats (Page 2)

1. What does "complacent" mean in paragraph 2?

2. How would a "complacent" or "indifferent" worker be dangerous? (paragraph 2)

3. What would someone think about the war if they said the war was "in the bag"? (paragraph 3)

4. Why does Roosevelt want his listeners to ask all the questions in paragraph 3?

5. Who is Roosevelt referring to in paragraph 4 when he says "Mussolini," "Tojo," and "Hitler"?

6. In paragraph 6, what does Roosevelt say the United States must do?

7. What is the overall tone of this Fireside Chat?

8. What is the purpose of this Fireside Chat?

9. How do you think Roosevelt's listeners might have responded to this Fireside Chat?

Name _____ Date _____

CHAPTER 7 ACTIVITY MASTER

Lesson 3 Reading Guide (Page 1)
Objectives: 5.1.spi.2, 5.5.spi.7
Accompanies Student Edition pp. 243-251

Part I: Vocabulary
Directions: Match the vocabulary word to its correct definition.

_____ 1. veteran   A. a silvery-white metal; source for energy at nuclear power plants

_____ 2. uranium   B. part of New Deal program to pay for college for veterans

_____ 3. GI Bill   C. a pause or break in fighting

_____ 4. atomic   D. having to do with atoms

                        E. a person who has served in the armed forces

Part II: People to Know
Directions: Write the word "true" or "false" to identify each statement. Correct false statements by rewriting incorrect information into true statements.

_____ 1. J. Robert Oppenheimer was one of the scientists who helped create the atom bomb, and he felt he had helped create something to save the planet.

_____ 2. Franklin D. Roosevelt asked Harry S. Truman to run as his vice president as Roosevelt ran for his third term for the U.S. presidency.

_____ 3. Harry S. Truman became president after Roosevelt's death and had to make the decision to drop atomic bombs on Germany.

Lesson 3 Reading Guide (Page 2)

Part III: Places to Locate
Directions: Complete the following sentences.

1. Anderson County and Roane County, Tennessee, were selected as sites for _____ because _____.

2. Oak Ridge was like normal towns because _____ _____. Oak Ridge was very different from normal towns because _____ _____.

3. The Japanese emperor surrendered after Hiroshima and Nagasaki _____.

Part IV: Short Answer
Directions: Answer the questions using complete sentences.

1. What major events happened during Roosevelt's fourth term in office?
   _____
   _____

2. How would you describe Harry S. Truman's actions in office?
   _____
   _____

3. How did the government keep Oak Ridge a secret?
   _____
   _____

4. How did World War II affect Tennessee?
   _____
   _____

Name _____   Date _____

CHAPTER 7 ACTIVITY MASTER

Lesson 3 Reading Guide (Page 3)

Part V: Memory Master

1. Who became president after Roosevelt died during his fourth term in office?
   _____
   _____

2. Describe the city of Oak Ridge, Tennessee.
   _____
   _____

3. What do the terms "V-E Day" and "V-J Day" mean?
   _____
   _____

Part VI: Constructed Response

Directions: Answer the question using critical thinking skills.

How was the end of World War II both a time for celebration and a time for mourning?
_____
_____

Part VII: Note Home

Lesson 3 Reading Guide is a basic overview of what the students have learned in Chapter 7 pp. 243-251. The Memory Master questions and the Constructed Response are indicators of student comprehension. For supplemental activities, see experiencestatehistory.com and click on Tennessee. Check with the teacher for the student login password.

Name _____ Date _____

CHAPTER 7 ACTIVITY MASTER

ELL: Taking Notes

Objectives: 5.1.spi.1, 5.1.spi.2, 5.4.spi.2
Accompanies Student Edition pp. 220-251

Directions: Take notes by writing the main ideas for each heading on the chart.

Heading	Notes
Axis Powers (p. 222)	
Allied Powers (p. 223)	
The Holocaust (pp. 224-225)	
Pearl Harbor (pp. 230-231)	
Tennessee Prepares for War (pp. 232-233)	
Rationing (p. 237)	
Women Go to Work (p. 238)	
Wartime Production in Tennessee Factories (p. 241)	
D-Day (p. 242)	
Roosevelt and Truman (p. 244)	
V-E Day (p. 245)	
Oak Ridge, Tennessee (pp. 246-247)	
V-J Day (p. 248)	
The Cost of War (pp. 250-251)	

© 2008 Gibbs Smith, Publisher
Accompanies *Tennessee Through Time: The Later Years*

Name _____   Date _____

CHAPTER 7 REVIEW

Chapter Review Study Guide

Objectives: 5.1.spi.1, 5.1.spi.2, 5.2.spi.3, 5.2.spi.4, 5.2.spi.5, 5.4.spi.2, 5.6.spi.1
Accompanies Student Edition pp. 218-253

Part I: Vocabulary
Directions: Study the following terms. You may also use your Lesson Reading Guides.

Allied Powers	dictator	Nazi	atomic
arsenal	Holocaust	racial supremacy	GI Bill
Axis Powers	hosiery	swastika	uranium
communism	inferior	liberate	veteran
concentration camp	lease	rationing	

Part II: Review the following ideas for constructed and extended response.
- Identify one reason Hitler rose to power.
- What actions did the Germany army take in Europe?
- Explain how the Nazi Party carried out the Holocaust.
- Why did Roosevelt talk about the Four Freedoms when he was re-elected in 1940?
- Who created concentration camps and why?
- Which three countries formed the Axis Powers? Which three countries first formed the Allied Powers?
- Who was elected president of the United States for a third term?
- What were some of the different points of view Americans had about entering war?
- What made the United States determined to declare war?
- How did Tennessee prepare for war?
- What did Americans do to help in the war effort?
- How did women's lives change because of World War II?
- What happened on December 7, 1941?
- Why did Americans ration during World War II? Name two items that were rationed.
- Summarize what happened on D-Day.
- Draw conclusions on how World War II affected U.S. and Tennessee economy.
- What major events happened during Roosevelt's fourth term in office?
- How would you describe Harry S. Truman's actions in office?
- How did the government keep Oak Ridge a secret?
- How did World War II affect Tennessee?
- Who became president after Roosevelt died during his fourth term in office?
- Describe the city of Oak Ridge, Tennessee.
- What do the terms "V-E Day" and "V-J Day" mean?
- How was the end of World War II both a time for celebration and a time for mourning?

CHAPTER 8 TABLE OF CONTENTS

Chapter 8
From the United Nations to the Civil Rights Movement
(Student Edition pp. 254-291)

Table of Contents			
Activity Master	Standard Correlation	Page #	Accompanies Student Edition pages
Lesson 1 Reading Guide	5.1.spi.2, 5.5.spi.5	134-137	256-265
Lesson 2 Reading Guide	5.1.spi.1, 5.1.spi.2, 5.2.spi.1, 5.2.spi.2	138-140	266-276
Passport to History	5.1.spi.1	141	276
Lesson 3 Reading Guide	5.5.spi.8	142-145	277-289
Civil Rights	5.5.spi.8	146-147	277-289
ELL: Themes	5.1.spi.1, 5.1.spi.2, 5.5.spi.8	148	254-289
Chapter Review	5.1.spi.1, 5.1.spi.2, 5.2.spi.1, 5.2.spi.2, 5.5.spi.5, 5.5.spi.8	149	254-289

© 2008 Gibbs Smith, Publisher
Accompanies *Tennessee Through Time: The Later Years*

Name _____   Date _____

CHAPTER 8 ACTIVITY MASTER

Lesson 1 Reading Guide (Page 1)
Objectives: 5.1.spi.2, 5.5.spi.5
Accompanies Student Edition pp. 256-265

Part I: Vocabulary

Directions: Use a dictionary to break each word down into its parts: root (or base), prefix, or suffix. Write the meaning of the word's parts. Then think of one or more words that have the same root, suffix, or prefix.

1. autobahn: _____

_____

Other words: _____

2. communist: _____

_____

Other words: _____

3. interstate: _____

_____

Other words: _____

4. satellite: _____

_____

Other words: _____

Name _____ Date _____

CHAPTER 8 ACTIVITY MASTER

Lesson 1 Reading Guide (Page 2)

Part II: People to Know

Directions: Write what each person did after World War II.

1. Gordon Browning: _____
   _____

2. Edward Crump: _____
   _____

3. Dwight D. Eisenhower: _____
   _____

4. Albert Gore Sr.: _____
   _____

5. Cordell Hull: _____
   _____

6. James McCord: _____
   _____

7. Alfred Nobel: _____
   _____

Name _____ Date _____

CHAPTER 8 ACTIVITY MASTER

Lesson 1 Reading Guide (Page 3)

Part III: Places to Locate

Directions: Locate and label the following countries.

East Germany
West Germany
North Korea
South Korea
Soviet Union

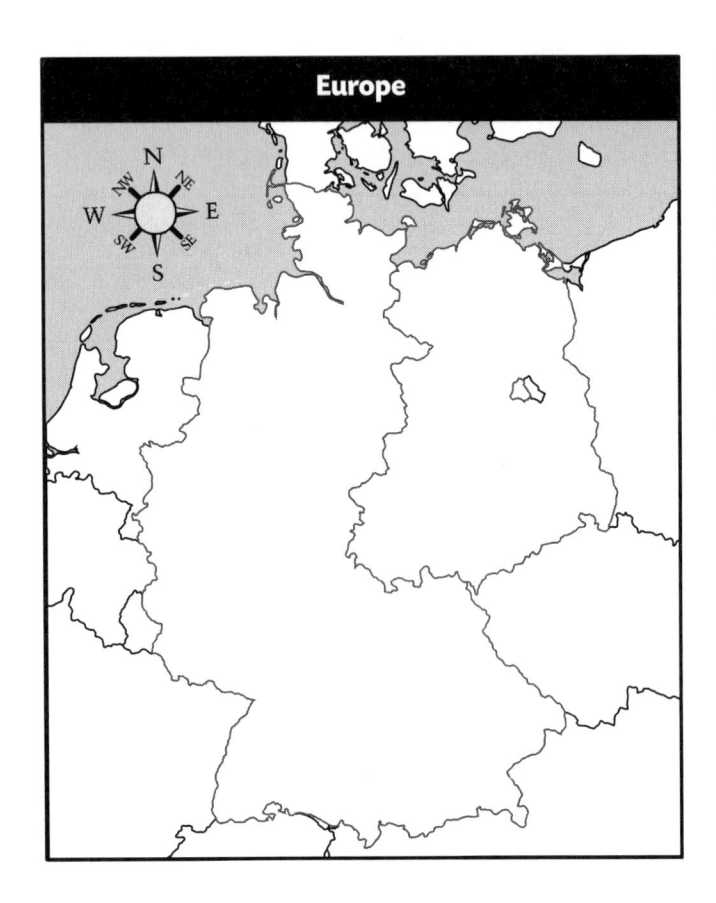

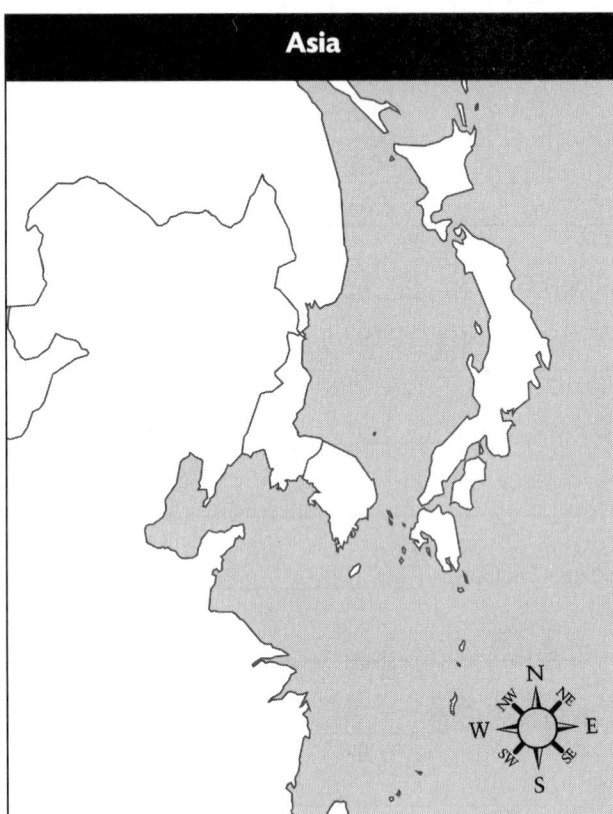

Part IV: Short Answer

Directions: Answer the questions using complete sentences.

1. Why was the United Nations formed?

_____

_____

2. How did the atomic bomb affect the Soviet Union?

_____

_____

Name _____ Date _____

CHAPTER 8 ACTIVITY MASTER

Lesson 1 Reading Guide (Page 4)

3. What was the Space Race?

_____

_____

4. How did the Korean War get started?

_____

_____

Part V: Memory Master

1. Why did Cordell Hull receive a Nobel Peace Prize?

_____

_____

2. Describe the Cold War.

_____

_____

3. Why did the United Nations send troops to Korea?

_____

_____

Part VI: Constructed Response

Directions: Answer the question using critical thinking skills.

How did life change after the technological developments of World War II?

_____

_____

Part VII: Note Home

Lesson 1 Reading Guide is a basic overview of what the students have learned in Chapter 8 pp. 256-265. The Memory Master questions and the Constructed Response are indicators of student comprehension. For supplemental activities, see experiencestatehistory.com and click on Tennessee. Check with the teacher for the student login password.

Name _____   Date _____

CHAPTER 8 ACTIVITY MASTER

Lesson 2 Reading Guide (Page 1)
Objectives: 5.1.spi.1, 5.1.spi.2, 5.2.spi.1, 5.2.spi.2
Accompanies Student Edition pp. 266-276

Part I: Vocabulary
Directions: For each vocabulary word, write the definition and draw an illustration.

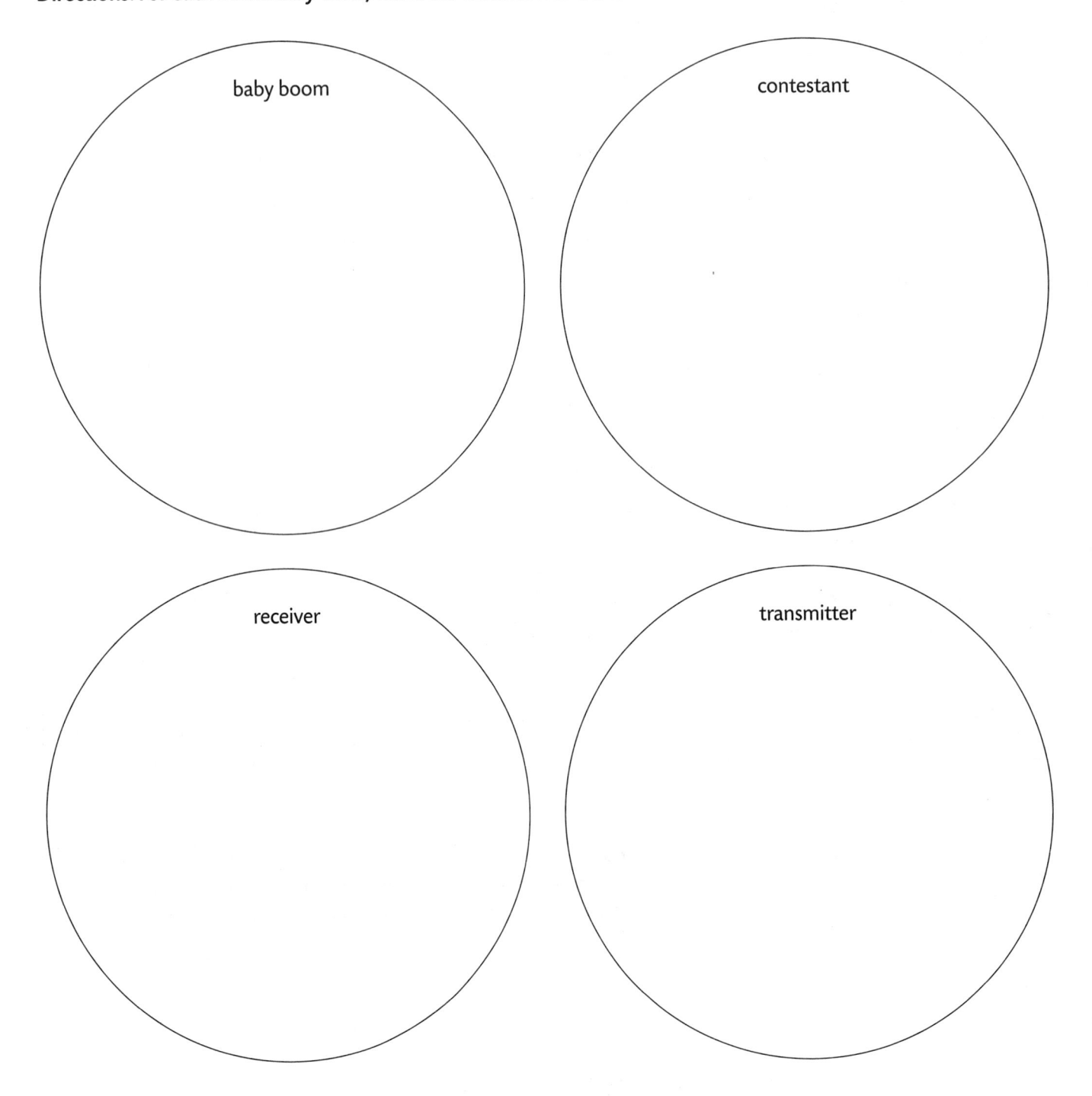

- baby boom
- contestant
- receiver
- transmitter

138

© 2008 Gibbs Smith, Publisher
Accompanies *Tennessee Through Time: The Later Years*

Lesson 2 Reading Guide (Page 2)

Part II: People to Know

Directions: Match the beginning of each sentence with its correct ending.

1. Groucho Marx was a comedian who
2. "The Blues Boy from Beale Street"
3. By advertising records on the radio,
4. Some of the early Sun Record artists
5. The King of Rock 'n' Roll is
6. Philo T. Farnsworth discovered
7. A recording studio was opened in Memphis

A. was the nickname for B.B. King.
B. were Jerry Lee Lewis, Carl Perkins, Johnny Cash, and Roy Orbison.
C. Elvis Presley.
D. by Sam Phillips in 1952.
E. recorded a blend of hillbilly and gospel music.
F. Randy Wood sold records all over the country.
G. interviewed contestants and gave them a quiz.
H. electronic images could be scanned onto a picture tube.

Part III: Short Answer

Directions: Answer the questions using complete sentences.

1. What is a consumer society?

2. How did television change life?

3. Describe the Tennessee music industry.

4. What made Elvis Presley a popular sensation?

Name _____ Date _____

CHAPTER 8 ACTIVITY MASTER

Lesson 2 Reading Guide (Page 3)

Part IV: Memory Master

1. What was the baby boom?
   _____

2. How did new forms of music, such as country and the blues, help the civil rights movement?
   _____

3. Why was the recording industry important in Tennessee?
   _____

4. What made Elvis Presley such a popular sensation?
   _____

Part V: Constructed Response

Directions: Answer the question using critical thinking skills.

Draw conclusions on how the music industry affected Tennessee economy.
_____
_____

Part VI: Note Home

Lesson 2 Reading Guide is a basic overview of what the students have learned in Chapter 8 pp. 266-276. The Memory Master questions and the Constructed Response are indicators of student comprehension. For supplemental activities, see experiencestatehistory.com and click on Tennessee. Check with the teacher for the student login password.

Name _____ Date _____

CHAPTER 8 ACTIVITY MASTER

Passport to History

Objective: 5.1.spi.1
Accompanies Student Edition p. 276

Teacher Initial _____

Date _____

Part I: Music

Directions:
A. Make a list of the new types of music that developed during this time.
B. Next to each one, write a sentence that describes how that kind of music changed Tennessee culture.
C. Write a sentence explaining how life would be different today if that style of music did not exist.

A. Music Type: _____
   B. _____
   C. _____

A. Music Type: _____
   B. _____
   C. _____

A. Music Type: _____
   B. _____
   C. _____

A. Music Type: _____
   B. _____
   C. _____

Part II: Constructed Response

Directions: Answer the question using complete sentences.

How and why does music change culture over time?

_____
_____
_____
_____
_____

© 2008 Gibbs Smith, Publisher
Accompanies *Tennessee Through Time: The Later Years*

Name _____ Date _____

CHAPTER 8 ACTIVITY MASTER

Lesson 3 Reading Guide (Page 1)
Objective: 5.5.spi.8
Accompanies Student Edition pp. 277-289

Part I: Vocabulary

Directions: Fill in the chart about for each vocabulary word.

Vocabulary	Write the definition in your own words.	Write a sentence telling how you use or hear this word today.
anthem		
civil rights		
discrimination		
evict		

Part II: People to Know

Directions: Write the one main area for which each person is remembered.

1. Oliver Brown _____
2. Mahatma Gandhi _____
3. Albert Gore Sr. _____
4. Estes Kefauver _____
5. Martin Luther King Jr. _____
6. Rosa Parks _____
7. Jackie Robinson _____
8. Gladys Stephenson _____
9. James Stephenson _____
10. Earl Warren _____

© 2008 Gibbs Smith, Publisher
Accompanies *Tennessee Through Time: The Later Years*

Lesson 3 Reading Guide (Page 2)

Part III: Places to Locate

Directions: Locate and label the following locations on the map. Then turn to the world map in your textbook (pp. 344-345) and point out India.

Columbia
Fayette County
Haywood County
Little Rock, Arkansas
Montgomery, Alabama
Topeka, Kansas

Southeast United States

Lesson 3 Reading Guide (Page 3)

Part IV: Short Answer

Directions: Answer the questions using complete sentences.

1. How did the Columbia Race Riot start and end?

2. Summarize the two sides in *Brown v. Board of Education*.

3. How did Rosa Parks's actions lead to a civil rights protest?

4. Explain what "The Little Rock Nine" means.

Part V: Memory Master

1. What was the Supreme Court's decision in *Brown v. Board of Education*?

2. What did southern politicians declare in the Southern Manifesto?

3. Describe the Montgomery bus boycott.

Name _____ Date _____

CHAPTER 8 ACTIVITY MASTER

Lesson 3 Reading Guide (Page 4)

Part VI: Constructed Response

Directions: Answer the question using critical thinking skills.

How did the United States confront the civil rights issues of *Brown v. Board of Education,* the Montgomery bus boycott, and "tent cities" in Tennessee?

_____

_____

Part VII: Note Home

Lesson 3 Reading Guide is a basic overview of what the students have learned in Chapter 8 pp. 277-289. The Memory Master questions and the Constructed Response are indicators of student comprehension. For supplemental activities, see experiencestatehistory.com and click on Tennessee. Check with the teacher for the student login password.

Name _____ Date _____

CHAPTER 8 ACTIVITY MASTER

Civil Rights

Objective: 5.5.spi.8
Accompanies Student Edition pp. 277-289

Directions: Read the following excerpt from a letter to students. It is a primary source from a 1960 sit-in that took place in North Carolina during the civil rights movement. A group planned to sit at a lunch counter at a store called Kress. Answer the questions that follow.

Pre-reading Notes:
- [sic] is a note that means this is the way the original document was worded and spelled
- agitators: people who stir up others on purpose; political troublemakers
- heckle: to try to embarrass or annoy others, especially public speakers
- partisanship: showing support or membership for a certain side

---

Dear fellow students,

A movement has been made on Kress' to obtain similar [sic] results expected from Woolworth. We are requesting that the students will fully Support these movements. However, we also request that no students shall go over the heads of the committee and start another such movement in that we must concentrate our efforts toward breaking down these places and we're certain that with success, the others will eventually fall in line.

As much as we desire the full cooperation of all students, we must insist that we show no violence under any circumstances. The insults received cannot harm us in anyway and any assault [sic] or any student will be dealt with immediately by the police department who have promised that there will be protection for ALL persons with no **partisanship.** We are asking that you will take no weapons with you such as knives, etc., but a Bible in its place.

The **agitators** who are **heckling** our group now are organized primarily for the purpose of "picking a fight." But if this happens, all of our previous work and desires are lost. Therefore, we beg that you shall completely ignore these persons and neglect the freak accidents. Keep a "cool" head and we're always sure of being in the right.

INSTRUCTIONS

(1) Students will wear dress attire . . . . (Young ladies are urged to look their best and gentlemen wear ties).

(2) All students going down will report to the Library dispatcher so as to make certain that we do not become so crowded until we [bother] the stores businesses. [sic]

(3) If the persons who arrive later or after the first shift has come, they will seek to relieve those who desire to be; if not, they will quietly check with the spokesman [sic] and then leave quietly.

(4) At no time will we fight back with words or physically, but will do so by our sitting.

We must remember that we are now well known in the eyes of the world and we must do nothing to hurt the chances of the minority races nor rob the people who sympathize with us of the loyal support they are giving us.

Again may we strongly advocate, NO VIOLENCE NOR DRINKING WHILE WE ARE DOWN TOWN OR IN THE EYES OF THE PUBLIC. We know that we will receive your loyal support in our drive for justice and we hope that you will weigh this letter carefully and cooperate fully.

STUDENTS EXECUTIVE COMMITTEE

FOR JUSTICE

Name _____ Date _____

CHAPTER 8 ACTIVITY MASTER

1. How are the students supposed to behave?
   _____
   _____

2. What are students supposed to do if someone insults or hurts them?
   _____
   _____

3. What could students take with them?
   _____
   _____

4. Why was this letter written?
   _____
   _____

5. Why were clothes important?
   _____
   _____

6. Who would read this letter?
   _____
   _____

7. What do you believe is the main idea of this letter?
   _____
   _____

8. What would make this sit-in successful?
   _____
   _____

9. What would give students courage to attend the sit-in?
   _____
   _____

10. Why do you think this type of protest was used more than once in places like Tennessee and North Carolina?
    _____
    _____

© 2008 Gibbs Smith, Publisher
Accompanies *Tennessee Through Time: The Later Years*

Name _____ Date _____

CHAPTER 8 ACTIVITY MASTER

ELL: Themes

Objectives: 5.1.spi.1, 5.1.spi.2, 5.5.spi.8
Accompanies Student Edition pp. 256-289

Directions: For each list, write the theme that goes with it. Think about what all the things on the list have in common.

List 1 Theme: _____

　Cordell Hull

　world peace

　countries cooperate

List 2 Theme: _____

　Soviet Union

　atomic bomb

　space race

　communism

　Berlin Wall

List 3 Theme: _____

　consumer society

　commercials

　Groucho Marx

　Philo T. Farnsworth

　transmitter, receiver

List 4 Theme: _____

　Grand Ole Opry

　ragtime and blues

　Johnny Cash

　Elvis Presley and rock 'n' roll

　recording industry

List 5 Theme: _____

　discrimination

　African American war veterans

　Columbia Race Riot

　Brown v. Board of Education

List 6 Theme: _____

　Rosa Parks

　Montgomery, Alabama

　NAACP

　Martin Luther King Jr.

　non-violent protest

　carpools, walking to work

© 2008 Gibbs Smith, Publisher
Accompanies *Tennessee Through Time: The Later Years*

Name _____   Date _____

CHAPTER 8 REVIEW

Chapter Review Study Guide
Objectives: 5.1.spi.1, 5.1.spi.2, 5.2.spi.1, 5.2.spi.2, 5.5.spi.5, 5.5.spi.8
Accompanies Student Text pp. 254-291

Part I: Vocabulary
Directions: Study the following terms. You may also use your Lesson Reading Guides.

autobahn	satellite	receiver	civil rights
communist	baby boom	transmitter	discrimination
interstate	contestant	anthem	evict

Part II: Review the following ideas for constructed and extended response.
- How did life change for the United States after World War II?
- Why was the United Nations formed?
- How did the atomic bomb affect the Soviet Union?
- What was the Space Race?
- How did the Korean War get started?
- Why did Cordell Hull receive a Nobel Peace Prize?
- Describe the Cold War.
- Why did the United Nations send troops to Korea?
- How did life change after the technological developments of World War II?
- What is a consumer society?
- How did television change life?
- Describe the Tennessee music industry.
- What made Elvis Presley a popular sensation?
- What was the baby boom?
- How did new forms of music, such as country and the blues, help the civil rights movement?
- Why was the recording industry important in Tennessee?
- Draw conclusions on how the music industry affected Tennessee economy.
- How did the Columbia Race Riot start and end?
- Summarize the two sides in *Brown v. Board of Education*.
- How did Rosa Parks's actions lead to a civil rights protest?
- Explain what "The Little Rock Nine" means.
- What was the Supreme Court's decision in *Brown v. Board of Education*?
- What did southern politicians declare in the Southern Manifesto?
- Describe the Montgomery Bus Boycott.
- How did the United States confront the civil rights issues of *Brown v. Board of Education* the Montgomery Bus Boycott, and "tent cities" in Tennessee?

CHAPTER 9 TABLE OF CONTENTS

Chapter 9
Civil Rights for All People (Student Edition pp. 292-323)

Table of Contents			
Activity Master	Standard Correlation	Page #	Accompanies Student Edition pages
Lesson 1 Reading Guide	5.5.spi.8, 5.6.spi.1	152-155	294-310
Passport to History	5.5.spi.8	156	297
Lesson 2 Reading Guide	5.6.spi.3	157-163	311-321
ELL: Decision-Making	5.6.spi.3	164-165	294-321
Chapter Review	5.5.spi.8, 5.6.spi.3	166	294-323

© 2008 Gibbs Smith, Publisher
Accompanies *Tennessee Through Time: The Later Years*

Name _____ Date _____

CHAPTER 9 ACTIVITY MASTER

Lesson 1 Reading Guide (Page 1)
Objectives: 5.5.spi.8, 5.6.spi.1
Accompanies Student Edition pp. 294-310

Part I: Vocabulary
Directions: Fill in the chart for each vocabulary word. Write the definitions in your own words.

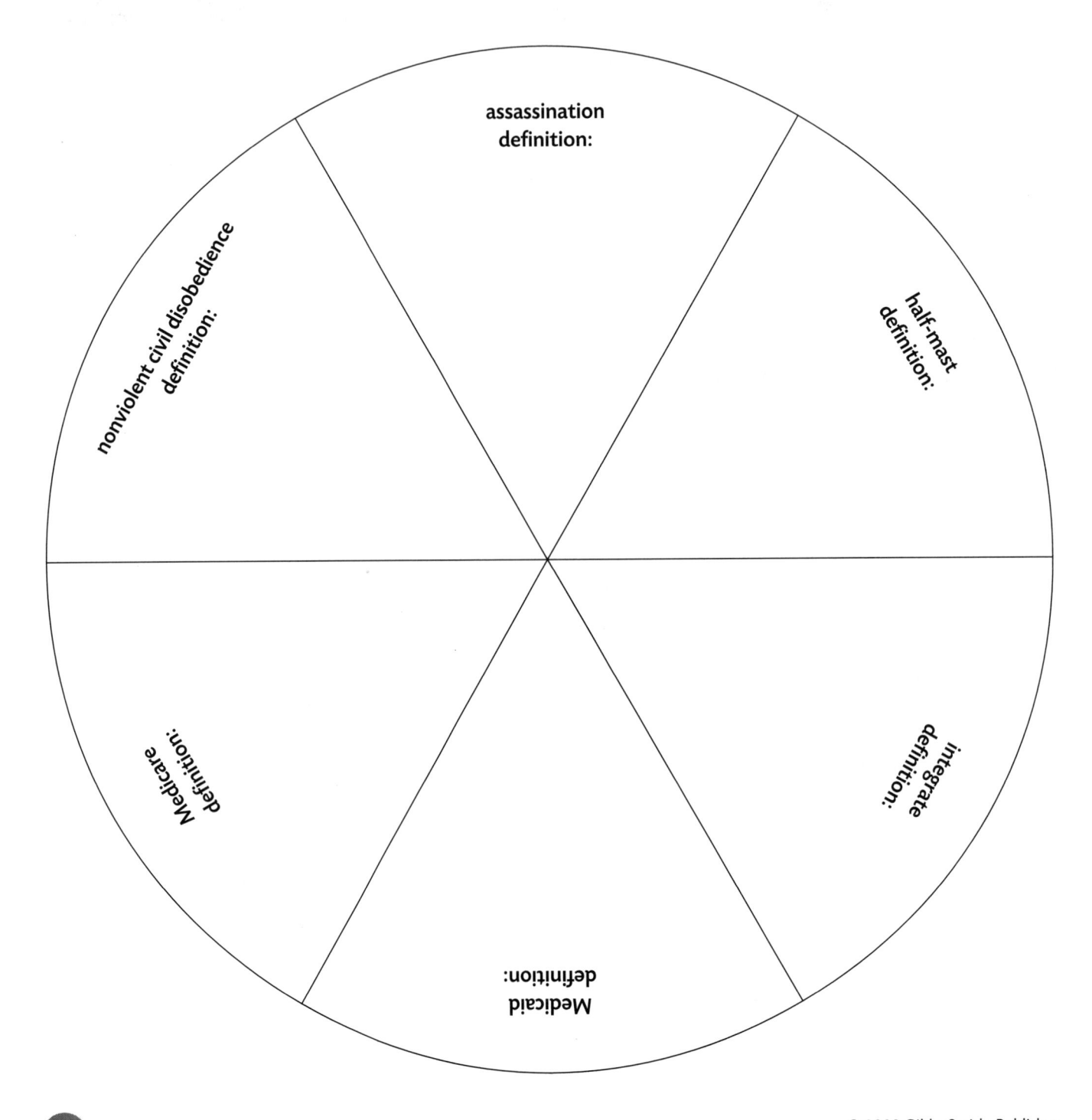

- assassination definition:
- half-mast definition:
- integrate definition:
- Medicaid definition:
- Medicare definition:
- nonviolent civil disobedience definition:

© 2008 Gibbs Smith, Publisher
Accompanies *Tennessee Through Time: The Later Years*

Name _____ Date _____

CHAPTER 9 ACTIVITY MASTER

Lesson 1 Reading Guide (Page 2)

Part II: People to Know

Directions: Determine if each sentence is true or false. Write "True" or "False" in the blank. Correct false statements by rewriting each one into a true statement.

_____ 1. James Lawson taught African Americans nonviolent civil disobedience he had learned as a missionary in India.

_____ 2. Diane Nash, a student at Vanderbilt University, asked the president of the United States if it was right to refuse to serve blacks at lunch counters.

_____ 3. President Ben West said serving blacks at lunch counters should be illegal.

_____ 4. The home of Z. Alexander Looby was bombed because he had served as a lawyer for black students.

_____ 5. Wilma Rudolph was the first female American athlete ever to win three gold medals at one Olympics.

_____ 6. James Earl Ray is known as the man who shot and killed Martin Luther King Jr. in Memphis, Tennessee.

_____ 7. Martin Luther King Jr. said he came to Tennessee to give people inspiration to get started in civil rights protests.

_____ 8. John F. Kennedy had introduced a civil rights bill that helped him gain millions of African American votes for his presidential election.

_____ 9. After President Kennedy was assassinated, President Lyndon B. Johnson passed the Civil Rights Act, but it did not include school desegregation.

_____ 10. Tennessean James Thomas Davis was the first American to die in the Vietnam War.

_____ 11. Richard M. Nixon ran as John F. Kennedy's vice president.

Name _____ Date _____

CHAPTER 9 ACTIVITY MASTER

Lesson 1 Reading Guide (Page 3)

Part III: Places to Locate

Directions: Answer the questions using the map grid.

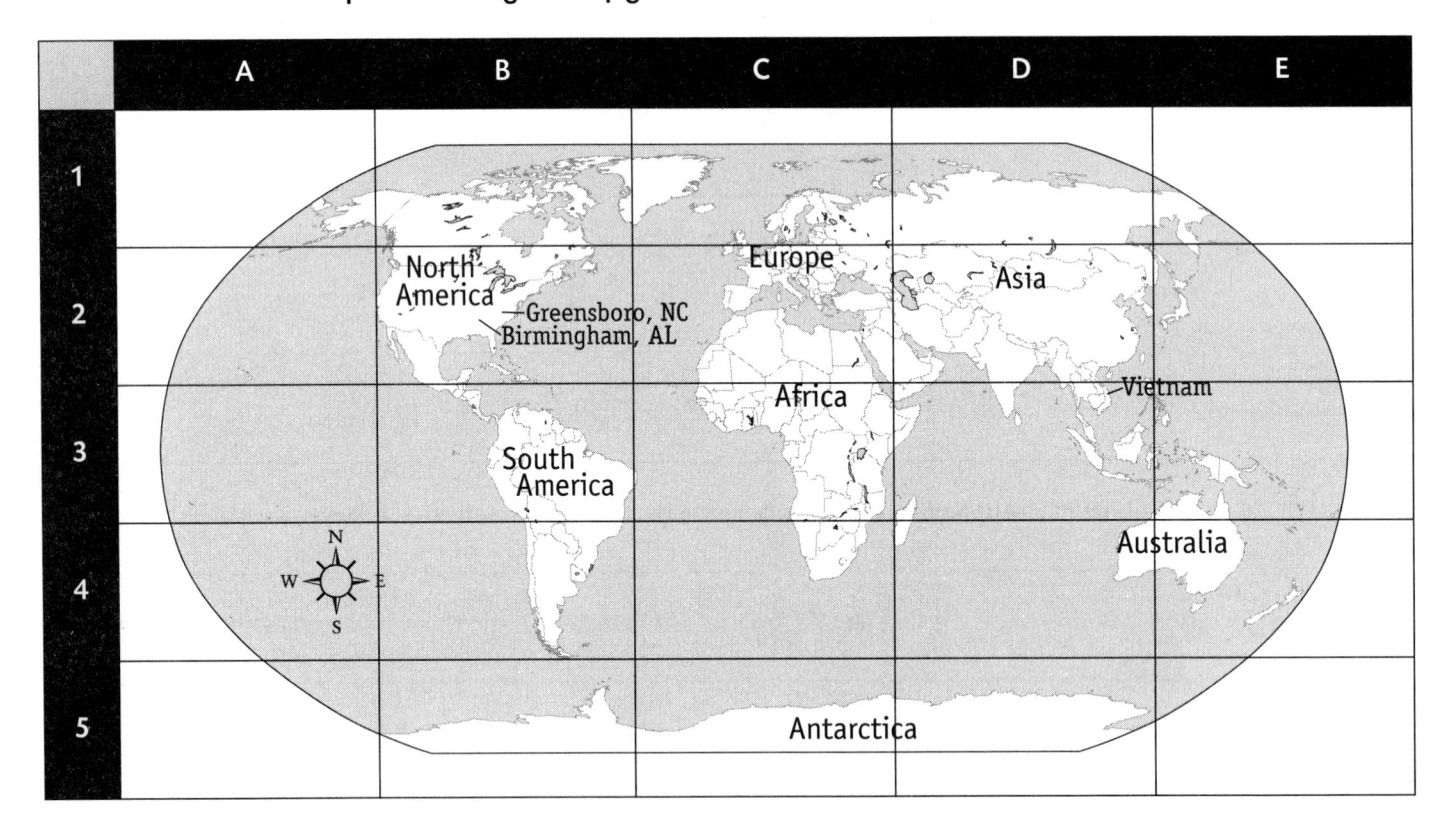

	A	B	C	D	E
1					
2		North America — Greensboro, NC; Birmingham, AL	Europe	Asia	
3		South America	Africa		Vietnam
4					Australia
5			Antarctica		

1. In which grid is Birmingham, Alabama located? _____
2. In which two grids is Vietnam located? _____
3. In which grid is Greensboro, North Carolina located? _____
4. Which two continents did you locate for #1-3? _____
5. How do grids help you locate geographical locations? _____

Part IV: Short Answer

Directions: Answer the questions using your textbook.

1. Describe a civil rights protest.

   _____

   _____

2. How was Martin Luther King Jr. influential in the civil rights movement?

   _____

   _____

© 2008 Gibbs Smith, Publisher
Accompanies *Tennessee Through Time: The Later Years*

Name _____   Date _____

CHAPTER 9 ACTIVITY MASTER

Lesson 1 Reading Guide (Page 4)

3. Describe President Johnson's "Great Society" plan.
   _____
   _____

4. Explain Americans' different reactions to the Vietnam War.
   _____
   _____

Part V: Memory Master

1. Identify two ways people worked for desegregation.
   _____
   _____

2. What was one of President Johnson's goals for his Great Society plan?
   _____
   _____

3. What does AIM stand for?
   _____
   _____

Part VI: Constructed Response

Directions: Answer the question using critical thinking skills.

How did civil rights gain national attention?
_____
_____

Part VII: Note Home

Lesson 1 Reading Guide is a basic overview of what the students have learned in Chapter 9 pp. 294-310. The Memory Master questions and the Constructed Response are indicators of student comprehension. For supplemental activities, see experiencestatehistory.com and click on Tennessee. Check with the teacher for the student login password.

Name _____ Date _____

CHAPTER 9 ACTIVITY MASTER

Passport to History
Objective: 5.5.spi.8
Accompanies Student Edition p. 297

Teacher Initial _____

Date _____

Part I: Viewpoints
Directions: Answer the questions by studying the photograph on p. 294 in your textbook.

1. Is this photograph a primary or secondary source? _____

2. Why have people gathered on the sidewalk? _____
   _____

3. Who is being arrested? _____

4. Why do you think he is being arrested? _____

5. If you were the man being arrested, what would you be thinking? _____
   _____

6. Why do you think the man with the white religious collar is walking with them? _____
   _____

7. Why do you think the photographer stood at this angle to take this picture? _____
   _____

8. Imagine you are related to the man being arrested. What would you think when you saw this picture? _____
   _____

Part II: Before and After Cartoon Strip
Directions: Think carefully about what happened before this picture was taken. Draw a cartoon strip showing a scene of what happened before and after this picture was taken.

Before	After

© 2008 Gibbs Smith, Publisher
Accompanies *Tennessee Through Time: The Later Years*

Name _____ Date _____

CHAPTER 9 ACTIVITY MASTER

Lesson 2 Reading Guide (Page 1)
Objective: 5.6.spi.3
Accompanies Student Edition pp. 311-321

Part I: Vocabulary
Directions: For each vocabulary word, cut out the card on the dotted lines, and fold along the bold line. Write the definition on the inside of the card. Draw an appropriate picture on the back of the flash card to help you remember the word's definition. For example, for "Hispanic" you could draw a map of the Hispanic countries discussed in this chapter. You can prop up the flash card on your desk or table to quiz your knowledge of the words.

bicentennial

terrorist

Name _____ Date _____

CHAPTER 9 ACTIVITY MASTER

Hispanic	cease-fire

Name _____ Date _____

CHAPTER 9 ACTIVITY MASTER

Lesson 2 Reading Guide (Page 2)

Part II: People to Know

Directions: Circle the people on this list who served as president of the United States. Then list them in chronological order from earliest to latest. For the remaining names on the list, write one fact about why that person is famous in Tennessee history.

- Ronald Reagan
- George H. W. Bush
- Jimmy Carter
- Gerald R. Ford
- Saddam Hussein
- William P. Lawrence
- Richard M. Nixon
- George W. Bush

U.S. Presidents:

1. _____

2. _____

3. _____

4. _____

5. _____

6. _____

Remaining People:

7. _____
   _____

8. _____
   _____

Lesson 2 Reading Guide (Page 3)

Part III: Places to Locate

Directions: For each location, fill in the chart. The first one has been done as an example.

Location	Continent	Involved in a war conflict in the 1990s?	Significance in Lesson 2
Afghanistan	Asia	yes	U.S. troops were sent here to fight terrorists after the terrorist attack in New York City on September 11, 2001.
Central America			
East Germany			
Iraq			
Kuwait			
Mexico			
New York City			
South America			
West Germany			

Name _____ Date _____

CHAPTER 9 ACTIVITY MASTER

Lesson 2 Reading Guide (Page 4)

Part IV: Short Answer

Directions: Answer the questions using your textbook.

1. What did President Nixon do to end the Vietnam War?
   _____

2. How did immigration policy change during this era?
   _____
   _____

3. Why was the Persian Gulf War fought?
   _____
   _____

4. How did Tennessee celebrate its bicentennial?
   _____

Part V: Memory Master

1. Why did Richard Nixon resign as president of the United States?
   _____
   _____

2. Which countries were involved in the Persian Gulf War?
   _____

3. What has the United States done to fight terrorism?
   _____
   _____

Part VI: Constructed Response

Describe conflicts with terrorism in the 21st century.
_____
_____

Part VII: Note Home

Lesson 2 Reading Guide is a basic overview of what the students have learned in Chapter 9 pp. 311-321. The Memory Master questions and the Constructed Response are indicators of student comprehension. For supplemental activities, see experiencestatehistory.com and click on Tennessee. Check with the teacher for the student login password.

Name _____ Date _____

CHAPTER 9 ACTIVITY MASTER

ELL: Decision-Making

Objective: 5.6.spi.3
Accompanies Student Edition pp. 294-321

Directions: Fill in the chart about each Decision Topic. Each chart has three parts: Possible Choices, Final Decision, My Reaction. The first one is done for you.

Topic: **Nashville Sit-Ins**	Possible Choices:
	1. Black students: Which lunch counters do we choose for the sit-ins?
Final Decision: Black students gathered and marched to the courthouse. Mayor Ben West declared the city's lunch counters integrated.	2. Lunch counter servers: Do we serve the black students?
	3. Black students: How long do we sit at lunch counters?

My Reaction: Though the black college students had to sit and do nothing day after day, it was worth it to have the lunch counters integrated.

Topic: **March in Birmingham, Alabama**	Possible Choices:
Final Decision:	

My Reaction:

Topic: **President Kennedy and Civil Rights**	Possible Choices:
Final Decision:	

My Reaction:

Topic: **Martin Luther King Jr.**	Possible Choices:
Final Decision:	

My Reaction:

Topic: **President Johnson's Great Society Plan**	Possible Choices:
Final Decision:	
My Reaction:	

Topic: **Vietnam War**	Possible Choices:
Final Decision:	
My Reaction:	

Topic: **Persian Gulf War**	Possible Choices:
Final Decision:	
My Reaction:	

Topic: **War in Iraq**	Possible Choices:
Final Decision:	
My Reaction:	

Name _____ Date _____

CHAPTER 9 REVIEW

Chapter Review Study Guide
Objectives: 5.5.spi.8, 5.6.spi.3
Accompanies Student Edition pp. 294-323

Part I: Vocabulary
Directions: Study the following terms. You may also use your Lesson Reading Guides.

assassination	Medicaid	disobedience	Hispanic
half-mast	Medicare	bicentennial	terrorist
integrate	nonviolent civil	cease-fire	

Part II: Review the following ideas for constructed and extended response.
- Describe a civil rights protest.
- How was Martin Luther King Jr. influential in the civil rights movement?
- Describe President Johnson's "Great Society" plan.
- Explain Americans' different reactions to the Vietnam War.
- Identify two ways people worked for desegregation.
- What was one of President Johnson's goals for his Great Society plan?
- What does AIM stand for?
- How did civil rights gain national attention?
- What did President Nixon do to end the Vietnam War?
- How did immigration policy change during this era?
- Why was the Persian Gulf War fought?
- How did Tennessee celebrate its bicentennial?
- Why did Richard Nixon resign as president of the United States?
- Which countries were involved in the Persian Gulf War?
- What has the United States done to fight terrorism?
- Describe conflicts with terrorism in the 21st century.

Part III: Timeline
Directions: Be prepared to answer questions about this timeline of events (also found in your textbook on pp. 292-

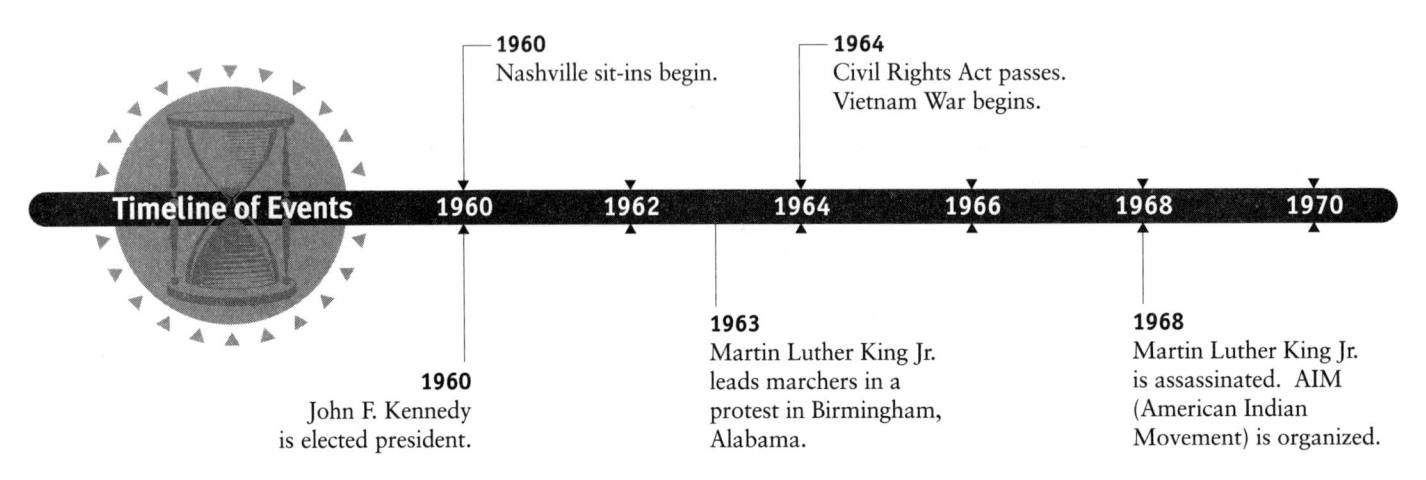

Timeline of Events — 1960, 1962, 1964, 1966, 1968, 1970

- **1960** Nashville sit-ins begin.
- **1964** Civil Rights Act passes. Vietnam War begins.
- **1960** John F. Kennedy is elected president.
- **1963** Martin Luther King Jr. leads marchers in a protest in Birmingham, Alabama.
- **1968** Martin Luther King Jr. is assassinated. AIM (American Indian Movement) is organized.

166

© 2008 Gibbs Smith, Publisher
Accompanies *Tennessee Through Time: The Later Years*

CHAPTER 10 TABLE OF CONTENTS

Chapter 10
Government for the State and Nation (Student Edition pp. 324-343)

Table of Contents			
Activity Master	Standard Correlation	Page #	Accompanies Student Edition pages
Lesson 1 Reading Guide	5.4.spi.1, 5.4.spi.2, 5.4.spi.4	168-171	326-332
Bill of Rights	5.4.spi.5, 5.5.spi.7	172-173	328
Lesson 2 Reading Guide	5.4.spi.1, 5.4.spi.2, 5.4.spi.4	174-178	333-339
Passport to History	5.4.spi.5	179	338
Lesson 3 Reading Guide	5.4.spi.1	180-181	340-342
ELL: Government Organization	5.4.spi.1	182	334-335
Chapter Review	5.4.spi.1, 5.4.spi.2, 5.4.spi.4	183	326-343

© 2008 Gibbs Smith, Publisher
Accompanies *Tennessee Through Time: The Later Years*

Name _____ Date _____

CHAPTER 10 ACTIVITY MASTER

Lesson 1 Reading Guide (Page 1)
Objectives: 5.4.spi.1, 5.4.spi.2, 5.4.spi.4
Accompanies Student Edition pp. 326-332

Part I: Vocabulary
Directions: Fill in the blank with the correct vocabulary word. Then write the **opposite** idea, or antonym, in the space that follows each sentence. Think critically to come up with opposite ideas.

graffiti	individual right	privacy	responsibility
income	intersection	property right	

1. Traffic lights are used at _____ to avoid crashes.
   _____

2. Laws to protect the things you own are called _____.
   _____

3. It is your _____ to obey the laws.
   _____

4. Money earned is called _____.
   _____

5. The Fourth Amendment calls for a right to _____.
   _____

6. Expressing an opinion is allowed by the Bill of Rights so that each person can exercise his/her _____.
   _____

7. Drawings on public walls or spaces is called _____.
   _____

Name _____ Date _____

CHAPTER 10 ACTIVITY MASTER

Lesson 1 Reading Guide (Page 2)

Part II: Purposes of Government

Directions: Follow these three steps for each purpose of government.

- Identify the purpose by writing it in the space provided.
- Write how this purpose applies to your own life.
- Evaluate how important this purpose is to life in Tennessee.

Purpose #1 _____

Apply: _____
_____

Evaluate: _____
_____

Purpose #2 _____

Apply: _____
_____

Evaluate: _____
_____

Purpose #3 _____

Apply: _____
_____

Evaluate: _____
_____

© 2008 Gibbs Smith, Publisher
Accompanies *Tennessee Through Time: The Later Years*

Name _____   Date _____

CHAPTER 10 ACTIVITY MASTER

Lesson 1 Reading Guide (Page 3)

Part III: Short Answer

Directions: Answer the questions using complete sentences.

1. Identify one purpose of government and give an example from everyday life.
   _____
   _____

2. What is the purpose of the Bill of Rights?
   _____
   _____

3. What are two examples of U.S. citizens' responsibilities?
   _____
   _____

4. Explain why the government collects taxes.
   _____
   _____

Part IV: Memory Master

1. What is one purpose of government?
   _____
   _____

2. Name one amendment in the Bill of Rights.
   _____
   _____

3. Which kinds of taxes does the government collect?
   _____
   _____

Lesson 1 Reading Guide (Page 4)

Part V: Constructed Response

Directions: Answer the question using critical thinking skills.

In what ways are everyday people, or citizens, part of government?

_____

_____

Part VI: Note Home

Lesson 1 Reading Guide is a basic overview of what the students have learned in Chapter 10 pp. 326-332. The Memory Master questions and the Constructed Response are indicators of student comprehension. For supplemental activities, see experiencestatehistory.com and click on Tennessee. Check with the teacher for the student login password.

Name _____   Date _____

CHAPTER 10 ACTIVITY MASTER

Bill of Rights (Page 1)
Objectives: 5.4.spi.5, 5.5.spi.7
Accompanies Student Edition p. 328

Part I: Matching

Directions: Match the amendment to its correct description.

____ 1. First Amendment   A. Soldiers cannot stay in your home during peacetime.
____ 2. Second Amendment   B. You may join and gather with any group.
____ 3. Third Amendment   C. The government cannot use unusual punishment.
____ 4. Fourth Amendment   D. Police must have a warrant to search your home.
____ 5. Eighth Amendment   E. You are allowed to own a gun for protection.

Part II: Purpose of the Bill of Rights

Directions: Read the Preamble to the Bill of Rights. Identify the purpose of the Bill of Rights by underlining it in the first paragraph. Look for why the states expressed a desire to add "further clauses" to the Constitution. Then answer the questions that follow.

The First 10 Amendments to the Constitution as Ratified by the States
December 15, 1791

Preamble

Congress of the United States begun and held at the City of New York, on Wednesday the Fourth of March, one thousand seven hundred and eighty nine.

The Conventions of a number of the States having at the time of their adopting the Constitution, expressed a desire, in order to prevent misconstruction or abuse of its powers, that further declaratory and restrictive clauses should be added: And as extending the ground of public confidence in the Government, will best insure the beneficent ends of its institution.

Resolved by the Senate and House of Representatives of the United States of America, in Congress assembled, two thirds of both Houses concurring, that the following Articles be proposed to the Legislatures of the several States, as Amendments to the Constitution of the United States, all or any of which Articles, when ratified by three fourths of the said Legislatures, to be valid to all intents and purposes, as part of the said Constitution. . . .

Name _____   Date _____

CHAPTER 10 ACTIVITY MASTER

Bill of Rights (Page 2)

1. Use context clues and the root or base word to figure out any unfamiliar words. If you need to, use a dictionary. Write the words you figured out here:

   _____
   _____
   _____
   _____

2. In paragraph one, what desire did the states express?

   _____
   _____

3. What might the states have been afraid would happen if they did not add the Bill of Rights?

   _____
   _____

4. Contrast the purpose of the Bill of Rights and that of the Constitution.

   _____
   _____

5. Contrast the purpose of the Bill of Rights and that of the Declaration of Independence.

   _____
   _____

Name _____ Date _____

CHAPTER 10 ACTIVITY MASTER

Lesson 2 Reading Guide (Page 1)
Objectives: 5.4.spi.1, 5.4.spi.2, 5.4.spi.4
Accompanies Student Edition pp. 333-339

Part I: Vocabulary

Directions: Read the clues to fill in the blanks with vocabulary words from Lesson 2. Write the circled letters in order at the bottom of the page to spell out a word.

1. political leader who works for the legislative branch
2. each branch shares equal control
3. different areas that a government oversees
4. governs Tennessee's state legislature
5. government in which power is in the hands of the people
6. an action that becomes a law
7. highest court in Tennessee
8. people elect them for Tennessee office
9. carries out the laws
10. writes the laws
11. decides what laws mean
12. governor says no to a bill
13. citizens who listen to cases
14. freedom

Write the word here in all capital letters.

_ _ _ _ _ _ _ _ _ _

Name _____   Date _____

CHAPTER 10 ACTIVITY MASTER

Lesson 2 Reading Guide (Page 2)

Part II: Tennessee Constitution

Directions: Read the excerpt from Section 19 of the Tennessee Constitution. Answer the questions that follow.

Section 19
That the printing presses shall be free to every person to examine the proceedings of the legislature; or of any branch or officer of the government, and no law shall ever be made to restrain the right thereof. The free communication of thoughts and opinions, is one of the invaluable rights of man, and every citizen may freely speak, write, and print on any subject, being responsible for the abuse of that liberty.

1. What are the "printing presses" spoken of in the first line?

2. What would you be doing if you were examining the proceedings of the legislature?

3. "...[N]o law shall ever be made to restrain the right thereof" of what?

4. What is "one of the invaluable rights of man"?

5. What should citizens be responsible for in terms of freely speaking?

6. What other document have you studied that is similar to Section 19?

7. When in your life do you exercise your right of free communication?

8. How is the purpose of the Tennessee Constitution different from the purpose of the U.S. Constitution?

© 2008 Gibbs Smith, Publisher
Accompanies *Tennessee Through Time: The Later Years*

Name _____ Date _____

CHAPTER 10 ACTIVITY MASTER

Lesson 2 Reading Guide (Page 3)

Part III: Three Branches

Directions: Draw a graphic organizer with information about the three branches of government. Use the information in your textbook p. 336.

Name _____   Date _____

CHAPTER 10 ACTIVITY MASTER

Lesson 2 Reading Guide (Page 4)

Part IV: How a Bill Becomes a Law in Tennessee

Directions: Write the seven steps of how a bill becomes a law in your own words. Use your textbook p. 337. Add illustrations in the boxes provided.

1. _____

2. _____

3. _____

4. _____

5. _____

6. _____

7. _____

© 2008 Gibbs Smith, Publisher
Accompanies *Tennessee Through Time: The Later Years*

Name _____   Date _____

CHAPTER 10 ACTIVITY MASTER

Lesson 2 Reading Guide (Page 5)

Part V: Short Answer

Directions: Answer the questions using complete sentences.

1. What is the purpose of the Tennessee Constitution?
   _____
   _____

2. What are the three levels of government?
   _____

3. What is different about the three branches of government?
   _____
   _____

4. Where does a bill go if both sides of the legislature pass it?
   _____
   _____

Part VI: Memory Master

1. What are the three branches of government?
   _____

2. Name one job for each branch of government.
   _____

3. How does the balance of power work in government?
   _____

Part VII: Constructed Response

Directions: Answer the question using critical thinking skills.

Describe the organization of Tennessee state government. What does each part do? Name one service Tennessee state government provides.
_____
_____

Part VIII: Note Home

Lesson 2 Reading Guide is a basic overview of what the students have learned in Chapter 10 pp. 333-339. The Memory Master questions and the Constructed Response are indicators of student comprehension. For supplemental activities, see experiencestatehistory.com and click on Tennessee. Check with the teacher for the student login password.

Name _____   Date _____

CHAPTER 10 ACTIVITY MASTER

Passport to History
Objective: 5.4.spi.5
Accompanies Student Edition p. 338

Directions: Write the purpose of each document in your own words below. Then cut them out and continue following the directions in your textbook on p. 338.

Teacher Initial _____

Date _____

Purpose of the Declaration of Independence

Purpose of the U.S. Constitution

Purpose of the Bill of Rights

© 2008 Gibbs Smith, Publisher
Accompanies *Tennessee Through Time: The Later Years*

Name _____   Date _____

CHAPTER 10 ACTIVITY MASTER

Lesson 3 Reading Guide (Page 1)
Objective: 5.4.spi.1
Accompanies Student Edition pp. 340-342

Part I: Vocabulary
Directions: Write a television news report that incorporates the two vocabulary words. Give your television story a headline.

local   sewage

_____

_____
_____
_____
_____

Part II: Locate Your County and County Seat
Directions: Use pp. 340-341 to point to your county and identify your county seat. Write the names here:

_____
_____

Part III: Short Answer
Directions: Answer the questions using complete sentences.

1. What types of services do local governments provide?
   _____
   _____

2. What is the purpose of county seats?
   _____
   _____

3. What is the purpose of county and city courthouses?
   _____
   _____

4. Identify one local political office. Can you name any of your local leaders?
   _____

© 2008 Gibbs Smith, Publisher
Accompanies *Tennessee Through Time: The Later Years*

Name _____ Date _____

CHAPTER 10 ACTIVITY MASTER

Lesson 3 Reading Guide (Page 2)

Part IV: Memory Master

1. Name two types of local government.

_____

_____

2. How many counties are in Tennessee?

_____

_____

3. What is a county seat?

_____

_____

Part V: Constructed Response

Directions: Answer the question using critical thinking skills.

Explain how government close to home works in your everyday life.

_____

_____

Part VI: Note Home

Lesson 3 Reading Guide is a basic overview of what the students have learned in Chapter 10 pp. 340-342. The Memory Master questions and the Constructed Response are indicators of student comprehension. For supplemental activities, see experiencestatehistory.com and click on Tennessee. Check with the teacher for the student login password.

Name _____   Date _____

CHAPTER 10 ACTIVITY MASTER

ELL: Government Organization

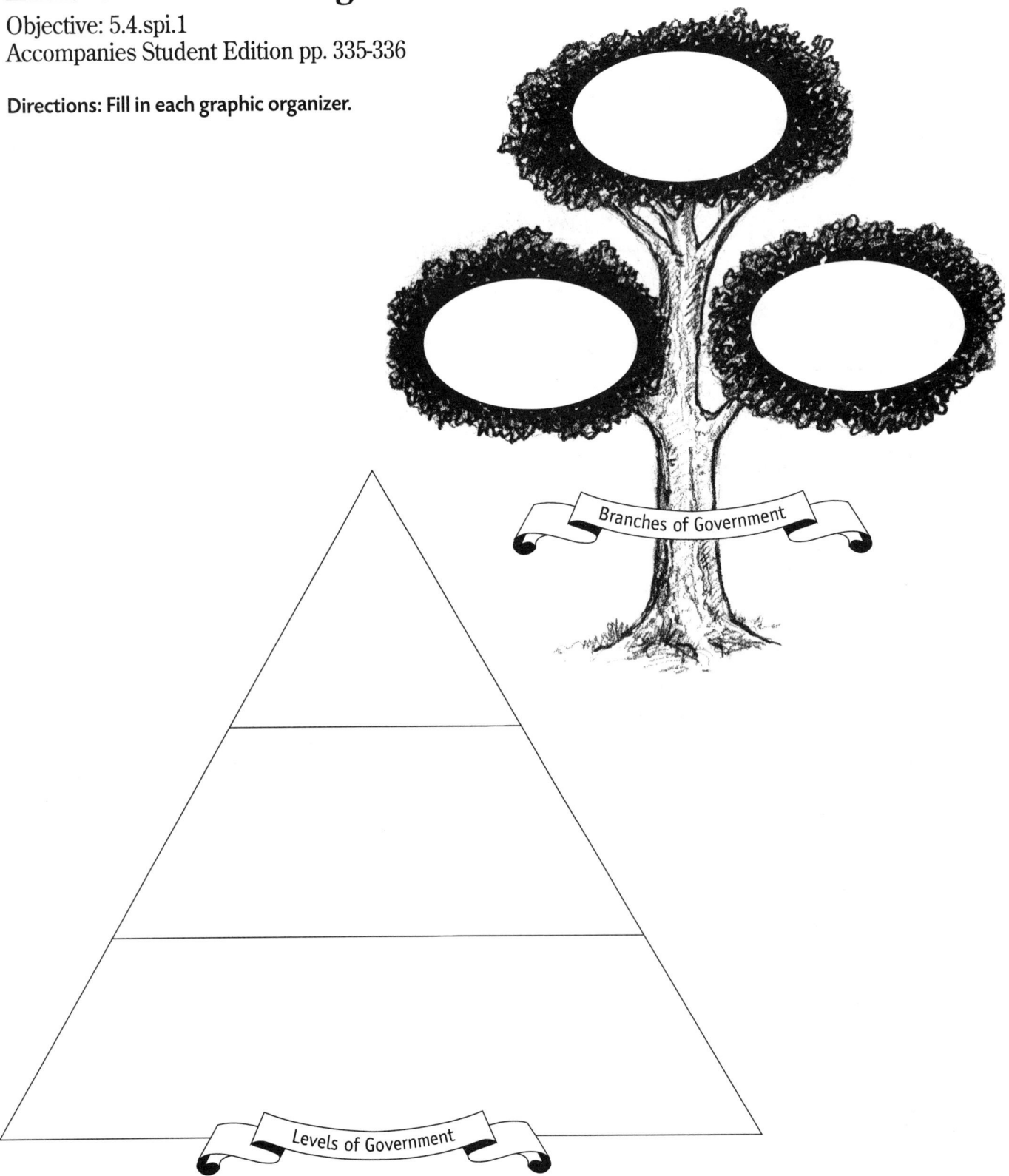

Objective: 5.4.spi.1
Accompanies Student Edition pp. 335-336

Directions: Fill in each graphic organizer.

Branches of Government

Levels of Government

© 2008 Gibbs Smith, Publisher
Accompanies *Tennessee Through Time: The Later Years*

Name _____   Date _____

CHAPTER 10 REVIEW

Chapter Review Study Guide
Objectives: 5.4.spi.1, 5.4.spi.2, 5.4.spi.4
Accompanies Student Edition pp. 326-343

Part I: Vocabulary
Directions: Study the following terms. You may also use your Lesson Reading Guides.

graffiti	responsibility	judicial branch	representative
income	balance of power	jury	supreme court
individual right	bill	legislative branch	veto
intersection	democracy	legislator	local
privacy	executive branch	levels of government	sewage
property right	General Assembly	liberty	

Part II: Review the following ideas for constructed and extended response.
- Identify one purpose of government and give an example from everyday life.
- What is the purpose of the Bill of Rights?
- What are two examples of U.S. citizens' responsibilities?
- Explain why the government collects taxes.
- What is one purpose of government?
- Name one amendment in the Bill of Rights.
- Which kinds of taxes does the government collect?
- In what ways are everyday people, or citizens, part of government?
- What is the purpose of the Tennessee Constitution?
- What are the three levels of government?
- What is different about the three branches of government?
- Where does a bill go if both sides of the legislature pass it?
- What are the three branches of government?
- Name one job for each branch of government.
- How does the balance of power work in government?
- Describe the organization of Tennessee state government. What does each part do? Name one service Tennessee state government provides.
- What types of services do local governments provide?
- What is the purpose of county seats?
- What is the purpose of county and city courthouses?
- Identify one local political office. Can you name any of your local leaders?
- Name two types of local government.
- How many counties are in Tennessee?
- What is a county seat?
- Explain how government close to home works in your everyday life.

Part III: Review
Be able to identify the three levels of government and the three branches of government. Review the purposes of the Declaration of Independence, U.S. Constitution, Bill of Rights, and Tennessee Constitution.

© 2008 Gibbs Smith, Publisher
Accompanies *Tennessee Through Time: The Later Years*